Voices of
the Industrial
Revolution

*Selected Readings from the Liberal
Economists and Their Critics*

Edited by
JOHN BOWDITCH and CLEMENT RAMSLAND

ANN ARBOR PAPERBACKS
THE UNIVERSITY OF MICHIGAN PRESS

PREFACE

As the title indicates, the book focuses attention on the economic and social issues raised by the Industrial Revolution. The first selections, from Quesnay, Smith, Bentham, Malthus, and Ricardo, reflect the views of men who were essentially protagonists of the new economic order. The remaining selections, Child Labor, the Chartists, the writings of Carlyle, Saint-Simon, Owen, Cabet, Marx and Engels, and the poets, voice the discontent of critics ranging from conservatives on the right to collectivists on the left. Some of the issues with which these writers were concerned are now dated, but the central question: "How can man best direct and profit from the forces unleashed by the Industrial Revolution?" is today more vital than ever, nor can one comprehend the ideological conflict of our time without reference to the founders of modern Liberal Economics and Socialism.

The introduction is intended to provide a general orientation to the topics treated, not a full interpretation or evaluation of the individual works. Brief biographical notes precede each selection. Spelling and almost all punctuation have been given exactly as found in the early editions from which the selections were taken.

JOHN BOWDITCH
CLEMENT RAMSLAND

SIXTH PRINTING 1968

FIRST EDITION AS AN ANN ARBOR PAPERBACK 1961

COPYRIGHT © BY THE UNIVERSITY OF MICHIGAN 1957, 1961

ALL RIGHTS RESERVED

PUBLISHED IN THE UNITED STATES OF AMERICA BY

THE UNIVERSITY OF MICHIGAN PRESS AND SIMULTANEOUSLY

IN REXDALE, CANADA, BY AMBASSADOR BOOKS LIMITED

UNITED KINGDOM AGENT: THE CRESSET PRESS

MANUFACTURED IN THE UNITED STATES OF AMERICA

INTRODUCTION

THE INDUSTRIAL REVOLUTION

The term Industrial Revolution was popularized by a nineteenth century English historian, Arnold Toynbee, who was impressed by the economic changes that had occurred in the last decades of the eighteenth and the first decades of the nineteenth centuries. More recent historians, looking back from the vantage point of what is truly an industrial age, object to the use of the term. They note that the characteristics attributed to the Industrial Revolution: the introduction of machines, new sources of power, the factory system of production, and the appearance of a new type of businessman willing to risk his own and others' capital, all either had antecedents that went back of the period chosen by Toynbee or came too slowly to warrant the label of revolution. They also note that Toynbee was an Englishman describing conditions that applied much better to the "Workshop of the World," as Great Britain was known in the nineteenth century, than to other countries that lagged far behind the pace setter.

All these objections are valid. The majority of Europeans of the early nineteenth century remained peasants living not too differently from the ways of their grandparents, and when Adam Smith described the manufacture of pins, he obviously had no conception of a Ford assembly line nor of automation. To anyone living in our day of billion dollar corporations and huge urban complexes, the world of Adam Smith appears old-fashioned, almost static. But compared to the world of the Middle Ages, what was happening to the economy of Europe in the period of the so-called Industrial Revolution did appear revolutionary. By the eighteenth century intelligent men, even if they had few statistics at their disposal, could see that that wealth was increasing, that the population of Europe was growing, that the application of science to technology was resulting in marvelous new tools and machines, that in place of a subsistence economy in which the family and local community supplied all its wants there was arising a more complicated exchange economy in which food and goods were produced primarily for sale in the market place. Most people might live in the country, but there was no blinking the fact that towns, especially textile and mining towns, were growing apace. Whether the term Industrial Revolution is a good one or not need not detain us. The important fact, for our purposes, is that the men of the late eighteenth and early nineteenth centuries found the changes going on around them a most challenging phenomenon.

MERCANTILISM

Medieval man spent most of his time and energy trying to feed and clothe himself, but one will search long to discover a Medieval writer whom we could classify as an economist. The reason is a simple one. So long as most men lived in a localized, subsistence economy there was no need to explain what appeared as commonplace facts of life. By the sixteenth and seventeenth centuries, however, the situation had altered considerably. The Age of Discovery and Colonization opened new world markets to European goods, creating something of a commercial revolution. At the same time the Tudors and Stuarts in England, the Bourbons in France, and other European dynastic houses were struggling to transform their feudal holdings into strong, centralized states. To do so a prince needed a royal army and paid body of civil servants, both of which cost money. The pressing question was how could the prince increase his revenues, and to answer that question there arose a school of political economists later called Bullionists, or, more commonly, Mercantilists. To appreciate the arguments of Quesnay and Smith, one must recognize that they were combatting the well-established doctrines of the Mercantilists.

The examples of success most often cited by the Mercantilists were Spain, the most powerful European state of the sixteenth century, and little Holland, which achieved an envious wealth in the seventeenth. The apparent source of Spain's power lay in her colonial empire and her fabulous treasure (bullion) fleets; Dutch prosperity was attributed to her flourishing trade. Observers in other countries, like England and France, concluded that the way to power and wealth lay through building colonial empires and encouraging commerce. Hence the Mercantilists advocated the building of navies and an aggressive foreign policy; they also urged state intervention to secure a "favorable balance of trade." They insisted that importation of foreign luxuries, which would drain money from the kingdom, be forbidden; that industries capable of replacing such luxuries or producing goods that could be sold abroad be subsidized; that merchants who could be induced to form trading companies, like the British East India Company, be granted royal funds and trade monopolies; that a high birth rate, use of forced labor, anything that would contribute to the war potential of the state be encouraged. By contrast, individual rights or preferences were of secondary concern. These statements may have a familiar ring. In the world of the twentieth century when "backward" countries are trying to jump the gap from agrarian poverty to industrial riches and war is endemic, Mercantilist doctrines are back in fashion.

THE PHYSIOCRATS

The eighteenth century provides a transition between the pronounced Mercantilism of the previous century and the triumphant Liberalism of the one that followed. Despite the great French Revolution with which it closed, the eighteenth century was essentially a period of political stability and economic prosperity, especially for the rising middle class. The Mercantilists had tended to view the wealth of the world in static terms. Eighteenth century thinkers were encouraged to believe that economic progress was possible for all. Above all, the eighteenth century was a period of intellectual ferment. The scientific discoveries of the previous century, crowned by Newtonian physics, captured the imagination of the *philosophes*. If there were natural laws that governed the physical universe, why should it not be possible to discover the laws governing politics, ethics, economics? A new faith was born; the faith that once the superstitions of the past were swept away and an age of reason introduced, there were no limits to what mankind could accomplish. With this faith was associated a new regard for the individual. The Mercantilists thought only of the interests of the state; the thinkers of the Enlightenment were champions of individual rights and viewed all human institutions in terms of the contribution they could make to the happiness, *bonheur* as the French spelled it, of mankind.

Quesnay* and the Physiocrats were not economists as we know the term. They used the title "Political Economy" which embraces a broader view of man than economic activity alone. In

*Biographical data and additional comments on the writers mentioned here will be found at the head of the selections from their works.

spirit they were akin to the *philosophes,* and it was fitting that Quesnay's first published works appeared in the *Encyclopedia* along with articles by Rousseau and the other moral philosophers. We have placed Quesnay's article, "Natural Right," out of chronological order because it best expresses what proved to be the major contribution of the Physiocrats, the notion, as Adam Smith expressed it, of "perfect liberty." By appealing, like most of the *philosophes,* to the natural order and harmony of the physical universe, Quesnay found the principle he needed to justify a free economy and an answer to Mercantilists. If he did not coin the phrase laissez faire — let things take their natural course — he and his disciples wove the concept into the fabric of late eighteenth century thought.

The distinctive feature of Physiocracy was the role accorded land as the true source of productive wealth. Quesnay's interest in agriculture was less odd than might at first appear. The Industrial Revolution was paralleled by equally impressive improvements in agricultural techniques. What we know as scientific farming had its origins in the eighteenth century, and France, the home of the Physiocrats, had the richest, if not the best tended, fields in Europe. Those readers who know the literature of the eighteenth century will also recognize the link of Physiocracy to the "back to nature" movement associated with writers like Rousseau. Finally, Physiocracy must be viewed in part as a reaction to French Mercantilist policies. Quesnay compared the famous French ministers, Colbert (1619-1683) and Sully (1560-1641), to the advantage of the latter. Colbert, he charged, had fostered artificial, luxury industries at the expense of agriculture and commerce. Undoubtedly Quesnay's remarks about the "sterile" nature of industry were colored by his acquaintance with those luxury trades for which the French, today as in the past, have shown a marked preference. It might also be noted that when Quesnay speaks of improving agriculture what he wants is a progressive, capitalistic form of production quite in keeping with ideas of the Liberal Economists.

ADAM SMITH

Liberal Economics owed much to the Physicocrats, but the true founder of the school was the Scotsman Adam Smith. Beside the *Wealth of Nations,* the writings of Quesnay and his followers, interesting as they are, appear fragmentary and half-digested. Yet Quesnay and Smith had much in common. Both shared in the cosmopolitan, optimistic spirit that pervaded the eighteenth century, and, despite the Scots' essentially pragmatic temperament, Smith too was more philosopher than professional economist.

The parting of the ways with the Physiocrats is strikingly evident in the first chapter of the *Wealth of Nations* where Smith describes the manufacture of pins. Industrial production, Smith argues, is admirably suited to the application of division of labor, whereas agriculture, by its very nature, resists specialization. The example Smith chose is an interesting one on other counts. Instead of selecting an article produced in factories, of which there were already many in his day, he took the pin, then still at the handicraft, small-shop stage of production. It was a good choice. If so much could be done with so simple an object, what unlimited opportunities lay ahead, what untold benefits would accrue once businessmen, freed of governmental interference, could apply the division of labor to all branches of industry.

In chapter two and later in the one on the Mercantilists, Smith deals with the nature of man as an economic animal. Here we find clearly expressed the basic postulate of the Liberal Economists that man, in addition to a "propensity to truck, barter and exchange one thing for another," is motivated above all by self-interest. "It is not from the benevolence of the butcher, the brewer, or the baker, that we expect our dinner, but from their regard for their own interest. We address ourselves, not to their humanity but to their self-love..." To quote Smith again, "I have never known much good done by those who affected to trade for the public good," and there is the famous phrase where he refers to the merchant, intending only his own gain, being led "by an invisible hand" to promote the general welfare of all. Even in the hands of the eminently practical Scot, economics cannot do without elements of mysticism and acts of faith.

The *Wealth of Nations* is so replete with quotable passages that text-book summaries are apt to leave an impression of dogmatism that was quite foreign to Smith's nature. The chapter on wages should provide a useful antidote. Like the other Liberal Economists who followed him, Smith opposed labor unions on the grounds that they interfered with the liberty of the individual and the functioning of the law of supply and demand in the market place. But Smith is almost unique in the frankness with which he admits that in the competition of masters and workers the advantages are all on the side of the employing class. The reader will also note the spirit of humanity with which Smith treats the subject of hours and working conditions. He appeals repeatedly to the enlightened, not the selfish, interest of the capitalist. Likewise the full text of his book would reveal that Smith was well aware that there are limits beyond which laissez faire should not be carried, and that principles sometimes must give way before practical necessities.

UTILITARIANISM

The ethical foundations of Liberal Economics were supplied by the utilitarians; in the case of the English economists, primarily by Jeremy Bentham. Like Quesnay and Smith, Bentham was a product of the eighteenth century, and the ideas he expressed were the common coin of the Age of Reason. His frank materialism, his lack of any aesthetic interest — "Pushpin is as good as poetry" — was perhaps unusual, but his faith in science, his constant appeals to reason, his life-long battle against all traditional values and beliefs were wholly in keeping with the spirit of the Enlightenment. What men seek, argued Bentham, is above all pleasure and the avoidance of pain; the end of all social institutions is the "greatest happiness of the greatest number." Futhermore, he could find no justification for shrouding the rules of individual or social behavior in mystery. One need only apply the methods of the mathematicians or physicists and tot up on the one side all the pleasures, on the other all the pains that would result from a given line of action. On the basis of this "felicific calculus" one could reach an empirically logical and mechanically accurate decision.

Bentham's impact on nineteenth century England was far-reaching. His disciples included some of the ablest economists and social reformers of the century, and through them his influence can be traced in nearly every act of "reform" legislation passed by the British Parliament. A champion of education, he gave an impetus to the agitation for schools open to the untutored masses; his faith in law as a means of social regulation encouraged prison reforms, the abolition of slavery, factory acts, and many other pieces of social legislation. In practice, the greatest-happiness-of-the-greatest-number principle proved to be a two-edged sword. Interpreted as the sum of individual happinesses, it could be made fully compatible with laissez faire doctrines; interpreted as the collective welfare of the social group, it provided an excuse for a broad area of government intervention. Bentham is properly linked with the Liberals, but there are elements of utilitarianism that appealed to the Socialists, as well.

THE DISMAL SCIENCE

With Malthus and Ricardo we move from the optimism of the eighteenth century to the deep pessimism of the first decades of the nineteenth century when Liberal Economics gained the title of "the dismal science." Malthus first published his essay on population in 1798 at a time when, as a result of poor harvests and war, food prices in Great Britain had reached unheard of heights and when the violence that accompanied the French Revolution had brought a revulsion against the ideas of the Enlightenment. Ricardo published his *Principles of Economics* in 1817 amidst the depression and social unrest that followed the Napoleonic Wars. What Malthus and Ricardo added to the body of Liberal Economic theory changed in no way the framework of the structure erected by Adam Smith, but the color of the walls had altered from bright to somber hues.

Malthus began his essay with the announced intention of proving the fallacy of eighteenth century optimism. The thesis he put forward is both deceptively simple and overwhelmingly convincing. Population, he argued, if unchecked tends to increase by a geometric progression (1-2-4-8-16), whereas the food supply, under the best of conditions, can be increased only by arithmetic progression (1-2-3-4-5). If, in the past, population and food supply had remained in relative balance, it was because of those "positive" checks provided by war, misery and vice, all factors entailing suffering for the mass of mankind. Was there any way out of the dilemma? Yes, one could apply "preventive" checks which Malthus lumped together under the term of "moral restraint." The trouble was that Malthus, and most of those who read his essay, had little faith in the willingness or ability of the common man to exercise control over his sexual appetites.

The essay of Malthus not only fitted the general mood of disillusionment that followed the French Revolution, it also provided the businessman of the nineteenth century with a most effective rejoinder for disgruntled workers who complained of low wages or those "do-gooders" who were constantly demanding measures to aid the poor and under-privileged. If wages were low, whose fault was it but the workers themselves, for were not the workers the ones who depressed the labor market by producing too many children? As for the humanitarians, who would maintain the poor laws and other forms of public assistance, was it not obvious that their efforts only compounded the very evils they wanted to cure? Did it make sense to tax productive wealth, the sole source of new employment, to support an idle poor whose very dependence on state charity encouraged moral laxity? It was a harsh doctrine to be fathered by an ex-minister of the gospel, but it was none-the-less popular with the advocates of laissez faire.

To the pessimism of Malthus, Ricardo added the cold logic of the theoretician who deals in abstractions. The selections we have chosen contain three of Ricardo's most controversial and influential doctrines: the theories of value, rent, and wages. Ricardo's labor theory of value, which postulated that the value of goods in exchange was based on the labor required for their production, a view also held by Smith, was later adopted by Marx in a somewhat different form. The theory of rent, in which Ricardo set out to demonstrate that in the "progress" of society all the benefits flow to the unproductive landlord class, stirred up a veritable war between middle-class businessmen and the "Corn Law" aristocracy. The former used the writings of Ricardo with telling effect against the landed interests whom they accused of selfishly using their control of Parliament to keep up the price of bread. Finally, in his so-called "iron law of wages," Ricardo combined the Malthusian theory of population with the law of supply and demand to prove that in the long run real wages would always tend to stabilize at that minimum level which would provide the worker with just enough to subsist. It is small wonder that with Malthus and Ricardo Liberal Economics, now come of age as a separate discipline, should arouse voices of protest.

THE SOCIAL QUESTION

By the second quarter of the nineteenth century the public became aware that the Industrial Revolution, along with such exciting inventions as the steam locomotive and the solid material comforts that accrued to the enterprising middle class, also had its seamy side. The first years after the Napoleonic Wars witnessed a major economic depression, and each following decade was marred by similar dips in the upward curve of industrial output. There were occasional bloody strikes and riots in the cities where workers fought to resist the introduction of machines. The towns themselves, as a result of rapid growth and lack of sanitary provisions, were often fetid breeding grounds of vice and disease. Furthermore, although many of the skilled workers were in a favorable bargaining position, other craft workers were ruined by the competition of machine-made goods, and most factory workers received what now would appear to be miserably low wages. Hours were long, ranging from ten to fourteen or more per day for a six-day week, and tens of thousands of young children shared the hours and working conditions of their parents.

The reports of the British parliamentary commissions appointed to investigate conditions of child labor in British mines and textile factories provide a kind of Hollywood dramatization of the theme of social degradation. There is no doubt that the testimony of the witnesses and the printed sketches of children crawling through the mine shafts were deliberately designed to impress the public, and the reports might well be placed in the category of social propaganda. Long hours and child labor, it should be noted, were not confined to the mines and factories; they applied equally well to the far more numerous home workshops and rural farms. The accuracy or objectivity of the reports, however, is of less importance than the evidence they provide that by the eighteen thirties and forties governments and the general public were becoming increasingly disturbed about the plight of the laboring class and the possible consequences of a continued policy of nonintervention in the economic sphere. Then, as now, if for different reasons, there was much talk about an increase in the crime rate and juvenile delinquency. What was euphemistically labeled "the social question," became the subject of newspaper editorials as well as of parliamentary debates.

In Great Britain and on the Continent the official investigations, backed up by public interest, led to the passage of child labor laws and to a few cautious, half-hearted efforts to apply state controls to the employment of adults. The advocates of economic liberalism gave ground reluctantly on the question of state protection for minors; they remained adamantly opposed to any legislation affecting hours and working conditions of adults. Laissez faire remained the creed of the businessman and the dominant economic philosophy of the nineteenth century. Until late in the century, remedial labor legislation came too slowly to promise a cure for the social problem. In the meantime critics arose who went much farther in their denunciation of the abuses of industrialism and who offered more far-reaching panaceas for the ills of society.

CARLYLE

In listing critics of the Liberal economists one naturally thinks first of those on the left of the political spectrum. In actual fact, some of the most effective voices of protest came from the right. The landed aristocrats, still an influential force in all European countries, were quite willing to champion child labor laws and other social legislation that applied only to towns and factories. In support of their position, they argued that the industrial slums were producing a deformed race of creatures unfit for military service and morally corrupted. A similar concern was expressed by many representatives of the established churches who found capitalism a godless, socially irresponsible creed. Social Catholicism, a movement largely dominated by men of conservative political and social views, owed its origins to this period.

Carlyle clearly belongs among these critics of the right. But Carlyle was no conformist or party man, and no single label fits him. He preached in the thunderous tones of an Old Testament prophet, yet he hardly belongs among the clerics. At times he reads like Edmund Burke with his pleas for a return to the Christian and aristocratic traditions of the past, but he also was unmerciful in flaying the dilettantish, Corn-Lawing aristocrats of his own day, and he talked vaguely of the need for a new class of Captains of Industry to direct society. Whether Carlyle, as some modern critics have claimed, was a proto-fascist, must be left for the reader to decide. What is certain is that no writer surpassed him in ability to lay bare the weak points in the utilitarian ethics and laissez faire practices of the Economic Liberals.

CHARTISM

The Chartist petition illustrates one form of left-wing and predominantly working-class protest. Although trade unions existed in this period, they were regarded as illegal, and they were too weak and undeveloped to obtain substantial benefits for the workers. Political action appeared to offer greater promise. The British Reform Bill of 1832 could be regarded as proof that political change was possible. What the Chartists proposed to do was to turn this minor concession into a precedent for the establishment of a truly democratic parliamentary government. Their principal methods were the holding of mass meetings and the collection of signatures to petitions which were then presented to Parliament for action. Today their demands do not look at all unreasonable. In fact, all have become a part of democratic practice; but to Conservatives and Liberals of the eighteen thirties and forties they were radical indeed. The violence that accompanied some of the demonstrations provided all the excuse the Government needed to suppress the movement.

Marx and Engels later asserted that the Chartist movement was the first true manifestation of revolutionary action by the proletariat. A reading of the petition throws some doubt on the validity of their claim. The style of writing clearly indicates the work of educated middle-class leaders, not that of simple workmen. Any reference to social reform, let alone to a radical transformation of society, if intended to be the ultimate goal of the petitioners, was carefully omitted from the text. The strength of the Chartist movement lay in working-class support, but Chartism remained essentially a political movement. In fact, throughout the nineteenth century the bulk of the workers, in England as on the Continent, exhibited far more interest in democratic than in Socialist programs.

THE "UTOPIAN" SOCIALISTS

By the time the Chartist movement was launched, Socialism had already produced a number of original thinkers and nearly as many rival sects. Marx and Engels labeled these early leaders "Utopian" Socialists, and for better or worse, the title has remained attached to them ever since. John Stuart Mill, the ablest mid-nineteenth century spokesman for the Liberal school, defined the word Socialism as applying "to any system which requires that the land and the instruments of production should be the property, not of individuals, but of communities, or associations, or of the government." Socialism, then, is a broad term, broad enough to encompass the Communists, or to quote Mill again, "those whose scheme implies absolute equality in the distribution of the physical means of life and enjoyment," as opposed to those Socialists who would admit some measure of inequality. The reader will find that the Socialists themselves wrestled with this problem of labels, but Mill's definitions remain useful both for the nineteenth century and later times. As for the word "Utopian," Marx and Engels intended it to evoke memories of Sir Thomas More's *Utopia* and similar works by non-Socialist thinkers who dreamed of creating ideal worlds. "Bourgeois idealists" was one of the milder expletives used by Marx to express his contempt for them.

Before suggesting the differences that distinguished Saint-Simon, Owen, and Cabet from each other, a word should be said about what the trio, and others of the school not represented here, had in common. All belonged in spirit, if not in time, to the eighteenth century. Like the men of the Enlightenment, they believed that man is a rational animal and that he need only apply his reason to achieve a progressively better life in this world. For the individualism of the eighteenth-century Liberals they would merely substitute the principle of mutual co-operation. There is virtually no hint of class strife in their writings and no appeal to revolutionary action. Instead they relied on the power of the pen and the power of example to win adherents. Rational men were expected to see the advantages of Socialism and adopt it by choice. With the notable exception of Saint-Simon, they appeared to look backward rather than forward in the sense that they wanted to replace the burgeoning industrial cities of their day with some sort of small, self-contained communities located in the healthy environment of the countryside. Like Rousseau, they would go back to nature. Finally, there is a strong religious element in their writings. Although dissatisfied with the Christian churches, they saw the need for some new religion of humanity that would weld men together on other terms than self-interest. The reader may agree with Marx that many of their ideas sound naïve and unrealizable.

CONTENTS

economic. Religion, philosophy, all ideological systems are mere superstructures or rationalizations erected by the class in power to justify its way of life. Ideologies change with the changing economic and political patterns of society. Where the "Utopians" saw society as essentially harmonious, Marx saw only class war. Medieval agrarian society, he suggested, was dominated by the landed aristocracy. With the emergence of a commercial and industrial economy, the aristocracy had to give way before the rising power of the bourgeoisie. Now bourgeois society was being challenged by the development of a class-conscious proletariat. No ruling class had ever abandoned its privileged position without a struggle; it was nonsense, said Marx, to believe the middle class would generously sacrifice the fruits of its victory. But the conditions of the struggle were changing. In the past, control of society had always rested in a minority; once the proletariat triumphed, the majority would rule and the basis for class conflict would cease. What a contrast in tone to Cabet's genteel *Voyage to Icaria!*

THE POETS

Throughout the nineteenth century novelists, poets, and artists raised their voices in protest against what many of them regarded as the crass materialism of the business class and the heartlessness of the factory system. Among the social novels of the mid-century one quickly calls to mind Charles Dickens' *Oliver Twist* and *Hard Times,* Benjamin Disraeli's *Sybil,* Victor Hugo's *Les Miserables,* and a host of others. They are too well known, too easily obtained to warrant inclusion. Most of the major poets, and many of the lesser ones, also took up the theme. The poems offered here have been chosen for the range of topics they treat rather than for the reputation of the authors or the quality of the verse. Those by Tennyson and Clough satirize the obsession of middle-class society with money; the "Song of the Shirt" by Thomas Hood depicts in moving terms the wretched life of the "home" worker; "The International," the hymn of international socialism, needs no introduction. The creative works of artists and literary men, if hard to evaluate, are an essential part of the social atmosphere of the Industrial Revolution. They add another dimension to the arguments of the Liberal Economists and their critics.—*John Bowditch*

It should be remembered, however, that these men were the creators of Socialism, that they were plowing furrows (or using spades) on untilled soil. It might also be added that their ideas are still very much alive. Modern concepts of city planning, for instance, owe much to the "Utopian" Socialists.

The diversity of the group is well illustrated by the three writers represented here. Saint-Simon perhaps should not be considered a Socialist at all. Except for suggesting an inheritance tax to limit unearned wealth, he had little to say about the distribution of property, and he is best known for his abiding faith in science and technology as the wave of the future. His demand that the direction of society be placed in the hands of scientists and technicians who would use their skills to the benefit of society is only by indirection a radical proposal, and many of his disciples, after a short period when some of them practiced communal living and were accused of practicing "free love," attained both fame and positions of considerable responsibility. They included such figures as the sociologist, Auguste Comte; the Liberal economist, Michael Chevalier; the banker, Isaac Péreire; the canal builder, Ferdinand De Lesseps. Even the French Emperor Napoleon III jokingly called himself a Saint-Simonian. A recent writer has detected elements of authoritarianism in the school; others have noted the parallel between the Saint-Simonians and the technocrats of the early years of the Roosevelt New Deal.

Owen was an associationist. Like the Frenchman, Charles Fourier (1772-1837), whose writings are not included here, he offered a plan for a model community (Fourier called his a *phalanstère*) which was to provide a maximum of individual freedom within a framework of social co-operation. The reader will note Owen's emphasis on environment as the key factor in shaping human character, a tenet fundamental to all Socialist thought, and his optimism, which stands in such sharp contrast to the dire predictions of Malthus. How a highly successful businessman could argue at such length for the practical advantages of a spade economy is but one of the many quixotic aspects of the group.

Owen was willing to leave some room for private property; Cabet would abolish it entirely. The only pure Communist among the "Utopian" Socialists, Cabet was quite prepared to see all the women in Icaria, his model community, obtaining their hats from a state-controlled store. His "Communist Creed" offers a fascinating mixture of terminology reminiscent of the Enlightenment—words like Happiness, Reason, Perfectibility, Natural Goodness—and ideas that were shockingly radical to his contemporaries. Cabet cannot be classed as an important or original thinker, but these two selections from his writings mirror well the idealism, the generous, humanitarian spirit of the Socialists of the pre-Forty-eight period.

MARXIAN SOCIALISM

Although the *Communist Manifesto* is not the whole of Marx, it is a good epitome of the Marxian doctrine, and there is too much packed into this short pamphlet to permit analysis in a brief introduction. The saving grace of the *Manifesto* is its clarity. Every sentence, every paragraph is loaded with meaning, but Marx and Engels were alike gifted with a flare for the trenchant phrase and the ability to simplify complex ideas. Anyone who will devote himself to the task can work out the main lines of the argument. It will suffice here to note some of the points that divided the Marxians from their predecessors, the "Utopian" Socialists.

First of all, it should be recognized that Marx owed a great debt to the thinkers of his own and earlier periods. He took a great deal of his economic theory directly from his arch-enemies, the Liberal Economists. He merely twisted or modified their ideas to suit his purposes. Likewise, he drew heavily on the philosophers and historians for his evolutionary concept of social development. In his university days he was an Hegelian and from Hegel came the dialectical method (thesis—antithesis—synthesis) he used to explain the process of historical change. Nor was he as far removed from the "Utopian" Socialists as he liked to believe. Many of the arguments he used against laissez faire capitalism came from their works, and he, too, was an environmentalist. One may well question whether his concept of the classless society, never spelled out in his works, was less Utopian than anything conceived by Owen or Cabet.

The split between the Marxians, who liked to call themselves "Scientific" Socialists, and the "Utopians" was based, nonetheless, on substantial grounds. Where the "Utopians" were idealistic, Marx was blatantly a materialist. The fundamental basis for all human actions and the foundation of every social institution, he argued, are

FRANCOIS QUESNAY (1694-1774)

Francois Quesnay, the leader of the Physiocrats, was the son of a Parisian lawyer and was, himself, a doctor, two middle-class professions that had little to do with economic theory and less with farming, that noble occupation so much admired by the Physiocrats. Much of his mature life was spent at Versailles, first as personal physician to Madame de Pompadour, then as court physician. Louis XV referred to him affectionately as "the thinker." He counted many of the noted *philosophes* among his friends, and two of his best known articles, "Grain" and "Farmers," written in 1756, appeared in Diderot's great *Encyclopedia*. These, and the *Economic Table* published two years later, made his reputation. One of his disciples, the elder Mirabeau, rated the latter work as equal in importance to the inventions of writing and money. Adam Smith, if a critic of the doctor's economics, paid homage to the originality of his views and to his pioneering efforts on behalf of the laissez faire theory.

The selections that follow are from *Collection des principaux économistes,* vol. II, *Physiocrates,* part 1, Paris 1846 (translations by the editors).

NATURAL RIGHT (1765)

The natural right of man can be defined loosely: *the right that each man has to the things proper to his happiness.*

We have seen that even in the state of pure nature or of complete independence men enjoy their natural right to the things they need only through labor; that is to say, by the effort necessary to obtain them: thus the right of *all to all* is reduced to the portion that each can procure for himself, whether he lives by the chase, by fishing, or on the vegetation that grows without cultivation. But to carry through such efforts and succeed in them, he needs the faculties of body and mind and the means or instruments necessary to act and to achieve the satisfaction of his needs. The enjoyment by men of their natural right is necessarily very limited in this state of pure nature and independence, where we can suppose no cooperation for mutual advantage and where the strong can unjustly employ violence against the weak. When men enter into society and agree upon conventions to their mutual advantage, they increase thereby their enjoyment of their natural right; and they assure themselves the full extent of this enjoyment when the constitution of their society conforms to the order clearly most advantageous to men, relative to the fundamental laws of their natural right.

But in considering the corporal and intellectual faculties and the other attributes of each particular man, we shall find great inequality in the relative enjoyment of the natural right of man. This inequality admits of neither justice nor injustice in principle; it results from the combination of the laws of nature, and men cannot penetrate the designs of the Supreme Being in constructing the universe, cannot fathom the ultimate goal of the immutable rules that He decreed for the formation and conservation of his work. Yet, if one examines these rules with attention, one at least perceives that the *physical* causes of *physical* evil are themselves the causes of *physical* benefits; that the rain which inconveniences the traveler nourishes the land; and if one calculates without prejudice, he will see that these causes produce infinitely more good than evil and that they are designed only to work for good; that the evils that they cause incidentally result necessarily from the very essense of the properties by which they achieve the good. The fact that the laws of the natural order are for the good of men accounts for their obligatory character; they impose on us the duty to avoid, so far as we can, the evil that we can anticipate through exercise of prudence. . . .

The transgressions of the natural laws are the most widespread and ordinary causes of the physical evils that affect mankind.

In order to understand the order of time and space, to regulate navigation and protect commerce, it has been necessary to observe and calculate with precision the laws of the movements of the celestial bodies; it is likewise necessary to know the scope of the natural right of men united in society, to determine the natural laws constituting the best possible government.

Men joined together in society must then be subject to natural laws and to positive laws.

The natural laws are either physical or moral.

By physical law we mean here *the regular course* of any *physical occurrence in the natural order clearly most advantageous to mankind*.

By moral law we mean here *the basing of all human action on the moral order that conforms to the physical order clearly most advantageous to mankind*.

These laws form together what is called the *natural law*. All men and all human institutions must be subject to these sovereign laws instituted by the Supreme Being; they are immutable and unbreakable and the best laws possible; consequently they form the basis for the most perfect government and the fundamental rule of all positive laws, for positive laws are simply laws of administration related to the natural order most advantageous to mankind.

Positive laws are the *authentic regulations established by a sovereign authority to establish the method of government administration, to assure the defence of society, to provide for the regular observance of natural laws, to improve or maintain the customs and usages introduced in the nation, to regulate the particular rights of subjects relative to their different stations, to determine the positive order in those doubtful cases that are reduced to questions of opinion or convenience, to settle the cases of distributive justice.* But the first positive law, the law fundamental to all positive laws, is the *institution of public and private instruction in the laws of the natural order* which is the supreme standard for all human legislation and all civil, political, economic, and social conduct.

The foundation of unity is the subsistence of men and the wealth necessary to provide the force to defend it; thus it could be only ignorance that would, for example, favor the introduction of positive laws contrary to the order of production and the regular and annual distribution of the wealth of a kingdom. If the torch of reason illuminates such a government, all positive laws harmful to society and to the sovereign must disappear.

GENERAL RULES FOR THE ECONOMIC GOVERNMENT OF AN AGRICULTURAL KINGDOM (1760)

II

That the nation be instructed in the general laws of the natural order which obviously constitute the most perfect government. The study of human jurisprudence does not suffice to produce statesmen; those destined for administrative careers must also be instructed in the principles of the natural order most advantageous to human unity.

III

That the sovereign and the nation must never forget that land is the sole source of wealth and that it is agriculture that multiplies it. For the increase of wealth assures that of the population; men and wealth make agriculture prosper, expand trade, stimulate industry, increase and perpetuate riches. On this source of abundance depends the success of all parts of the administration of the kingdom.

IV

That property rights in land and personal wealth be guaranteed to those who possess them legitimately; BECAUSE THE SECURITY OF PROPERTY IS THE ESSENTIAL FOUNDATION OF THE ECONOMIC STRUCTURE OF SOCIETY. Without security of property the land will remain uncultivated. There will be neither proprietors nor farmers to lay out the funds for improvements and to cultivate the land if protection of property and the returns from it cannot be assured to those who make such investments. It is the security of permanent ownership that encourages men to effort and to the use of capital to improve the output of the land and of commercial and industrial enterprises, as well.

V

That taxes should not be destructive nor out of proportion to the sum total of the national revenue; that any increase be dependent on an increase of the revenue; that it be levied directly on the net product of the land, and not on salaries, nor on necessities, where it would multiply the expenses of collection, would be prejudicial to trade, and would annually wipe out a part of the wealth of the nation. Nor should taxes be levied on the capital of the cultivators of land, BECAUSE THE ADVANCES OF AGRICULTURE SHOULD BE CONSIDERED A PERMANENT FUND THAT MUST BE CAREFULLY PRESERVED FOR THE PRODUCTION OF TAXES, REVENUES, AND THE SUBSISTENCE OF ALL CLASSES OF CITIZENS: otherwise taxation degenerates into spoliation and causes a decline that promptly brings ruin to the state.

VIII

That political economy should be concerned only with productive expenditures and trade in raw produce, and that it should follow a hands-off policy with regard to sterile expenditures.

IX

That a nation with a substantial area of agricultural land and the facilities to carry on an extensive trade in raw produce should not encourage too far the use of money and men in the manufacturing and trade of luxury goods to the prejudice of work and expenditures on agriculture; for, above all, THE KINGDOM SHOULD BE WELL POPULATED WITH WELL-TO-DO CULTIVATORS OF THE SOIL.

XII

That the children of prosperous farmers should remain in the country to perpetuate the labor force; for if discontent leads them to abandon the fields and to move into the cities, they carry with them the wealth of their parents that had been employed in cultivation of the soil. IT IS LESS MEN THAN CAPITAL THAT MUST BE ATTRACTED TO THE FIELDS; for the more wealth is invested in cultivation, the less manpower is needed, the more it prospers and the greater the yield in income. Such, for example, is the case for large-scale production of grain by rich farmers compared to the small-scale production of poor share-croppers who work with oxen or cows.

XIII

That each should be free to raise on his land such products as his self-interest, or his abilities and the nature of the soil suggest as most profitable. One ought not to encourage monopoly in agriculture, for it is prejudicial to the general revenue of the nation. The prejudice which leads to favoring an abundance of basic foodstuffs at the expense of other products . . . is inspired by a short-range view that fails to take into account the reciprocal influence of foreign trade . . . which determines the price of those foodstuffs which each nation can cultivate with the greatest advantage.

XIV

That the increase of livestock should be encouraged, because these animals provide the manure that makes possible rich harvests.

XV

That the lands employed for raising grain should be combined, as far as possible, in large holdings worked by well-to-do farmers, for there is less expenditure required for the maintenance and repair of buildings and proportionately much less expense and much greater net return in large agricultural enterprises than in small ones. . . . Any labor saving that can be achieved by use of animals, machines, water power, etc., redounds to the advantage of the whole population, because a greater net produce secures a large profit that becomes available for other services and activities.

XVI

That international trade in raw produce should not be prohibited, FOR THE EXTENT OF THE MARKET DETERMINES PRODUCTION.

$S - D$

XIX

That one should not consider cheap food an advantage to the populace, because cheap food reduces the wages of the workers, lowers their standard of living, provides less work and profitable employment, and destroys the revenues of the nation.

XXIV

That one should not be deceived by an apparent favorable balance in foreign trade simply by measuring the monetary balance and without examining the greater or smaller profit yielded by the goods bought and sold. For often the nation which receives a surplus of money is the loser, and this loss affects adversely the distribution and reproduction of national income.

XXV

That complete freedom of trade should be maintained, FOR THE SAFEST REGULATION OF INTERNAL AND EXTERNAL TRADE, THE MOST EXACT, THE MOST PROFITABLE TO THE NATION AND STATE, RESULTS FROM COMPLETE FREEDOM OF COMPETITION.

ANALYSIS OF THE ECONOMIC TABLE (1760)

The nation consists of three classes of citizens: the *productive class,* the *proprietary class,* and the *sterile class.*

The *productive class* is the one that creates, by cultivation of the land, the annual riches of the nation, that advances the cost of agricultural improvements, and that pays annually the revenues of the proprietors of land. One includes in the responsibility of this class all the works and all the expenses which are expended up to the initial sale of the produce; it is from this sale that one knows the value of the annual reproduction of wealth of the nation.

The *class of the proprietors* includes the sovereign, the owners of land, and the collectors of tithes. This class subsists on the revenue or net product of cultivation, which is paid annually by the productive class after the latter has withdrawn from the annual harvest the amount needed to reimburse it for the annual expenditures required to pay the costs of exploitation.

The _sterile class_ consists of all citizens occupied in services and works other than those of agriculture, and whose expenses are paid by the productive class and the class of proprietors who themselves draw their resources from the productive class.

GRAIN (1756)

The principal objects of commerce in France are grains, wines and spirits, salt, flax and linens, wool and other products furnished by animals. The manufacture of cloth and common fabrics could greatly increase the value of flax, linen, and wool, and provide subsistence for many men who would be advantageously employed in such work. But one perceives today that the production and trade of most of these commodities are almost extinguished in France. For a long time the manufacture of luxuries has seduced the nation; we have neither the silk nor the wools appropriate to fabricating beautiful fabrics and fine cloth; we have delivered ourselves up to an industry that is foreign to us; and we have employed in it a multitude of men at a time when the kingdom was being depopulated and when the fields were being abandoned. They have lowered the price of our wheat in order that manufacture and manual labor should be less dear than abroad; men and wealth have concentrated in the cities; agriculture, the most fruitful and noblest part of our commerce, the source of the revenue of the kingdom, has not been recognized as the foundation of our wealth; it has apparently interested only the farmer and peasant. Attention has been paid solely to the subsistence of the nation which, through the purchase of necessities, pays the cost of cultivation; and they have believed that it was commerce or exchange based on industry that brings gold and silver into the kingdom. They have forbidden the planting of vines; they have urged the cultivation of mulberry bushes; they have hampered the sale of agricultural products and diminished the revenue from the land to favor manufactures prejudicial to our proper commerce.

France can produce in abundance all essentials; it need purchase abroad only luxury goods. Mutual exchange between nations is necessary to maintain commerce; but we are principally concerned with the fabrication and sale of objects that we could

obtain abroad; and, by a commerce characterized by too restricted competition, we have tried to injure our neighbors and
to deprive them of the income that they might obtain from us
by the sale of their merchandise.

By this policy we have destroyed a reciprocal trade that
was greatly to our advantage; they have closed off their markets
to our goods, and we buy from them, through smuggling and at
high cost, the raw materials that we employ in our manufactures. In order to earn a few millions to fabricate and sell some
fancy goods, we have lost billions on the product of our land;
and the nation, decked out in gold and silver tinsel, has believed
it was enjoying a flourishing commerce.

The consumption of goods by his subjects is the source of
the revenues of the sovereign; and the sale of the surplus to the
foreigner increases the wealth of the people. The prosperity of
the state depends on the concurrence of these two advantages; but
consumption sustained by luxuries is too limited; it can maintain
itself only by opulence; men of modest means can indulge in it
only to their prejudice and to the disadvantage of the state.

The ministry, today more enlightened, knows that the consumption which can procure great revenues to the sovereign, and
which provides the well being of his subjects, is that general consumption which satisfies the needs of life. It is only indigence
that can reduce us to drinking water, to eating bad bread, and to
clothing ourselves with rags; all men try by their labor to procure
good food, good clothing. One cannot encourage their efforts too
far, for the profits and expenditures of the people are the revenues
of the kingdom and provide the wealth of the sovereign.

The detail into which we are going to enter on the revenues
that can procure abundant harvests of grain, and on the liberty
in the trade of this commodity will prove sufficiently how the
production of products of primary necessity, their sale and consumption, interest all classes of the kingdom and will make it
possible to judge what one ought to expect today with regard to
government policy on the re-establishment of agriculture.

The re-establishment of our cultivation supposes also the
increase of the population; the progress of the one and the other
ought to go together. Thus it is necessary that internal consumption and sales abroad tend to a certain increase in the price
of grains. The sale to the foreigner facilitates turn-over, encour-

ages cultivation, and increases the revenues from the land; the increase of income leads to increased expenditures which favors population, because the increase of expenditures provides profits for a larger number of men. . . .

But all these increases can begin only with the increase of revenues. That is the essential point and the one most ignored or, at least, most neglected in France; they have not even recognized, in the employment of men, the difference between the value of enterprises that return only the price of the manual labor and of those that pay the manual labor and still produce a surplus. Because of this oversight, they have preferred industry to agriculture and commerce in manufactured goods to commerce in indigenous products; they have even supported manufactures and trade in luxuries to the prejudice of the cultivation of the land.

Yet it is evident that the only means available to the government to make commerce flourish and to sustain and extend industry is to achieve an increase of revenues; because these revenues alone call into being the merchants and artisans and pay for their services. It is necessary, then, to cultivate the base of the tree and not to limit oneself to trimming the branches; let us leave them to arrange themselves and to spread freely; but let us not neglect the land which furnishes the necessary sap for their nourishment and growth. M. Colbert, too concerned with manufactures, still recognized that it was necessary to lower the land tax (*taille*) and make some advances to the cultivator in order to assist an agriculture that was perishing because he could not conciliate it with the needs of the state; but he did not mention the essential means which consisted in subjecting the land tax to a fair levy and in establishing full liberty of trade in grains. Agriculture was neglected; the wars which were continuous, the militia which depopulated the countryside diminished the revenues of the kingdom. . . .

One cannot too much admire the superiority of views of M. de Sully: that great minister had seized the true principles of the economic government of the realm by establishing the power of the state, the happiness of the people, on the revenues of the land; that is to say, on agriculture and on the foreign sale of its products; he said that without export of wheat the subjects would soon be without money and the sovereign without revenues. The supposed advantages of manufacturers of all kinds had not seduced him; he protected only those of woolens because he recognized that the abundance of the harvest depended on the sale of wool which favors the multiplication of flocks necessary to fertilize the land.

The lands cultivated in plots by small farmers demand more men and expense and the profits are much more limited. Now, men and expenditures must not be wasted in works which could be more profitable to the state if executed with fewer men and less expense. This bad use of men for cultivation of the land would be prejudicial even in a highly populated kingdom; because the more it is populated, the more necessary it is to derive a large return from the land; but it would be still more disadvantageous in an under-populated kingdom, because then it would be necessary to pay more attention to distributing the men among those enterprises that were most essential and most profitable to the nation. The advantages of agriculture depend heavily, then, on combining lands into large farms, put in the best state of cultivation by rich farmers.

The cultivation which can be executed only with human labor is that of the vine; it could occupy a larger number of men in France if the sale of wine was favored and if the population increased. The culture of and trade in wines and spirits are too much hampered; it is, however, a subject that merits less attention than the cultivation of grains.

We do not envisage the rich farmer as a worker who himself works the land; he is an entrepreneur who directs and gives value to his enterprise by his intelligence and wealth. Agriculture carried on by rich cultivators is a very honest and lucrative profession, reserved to free men able to advance the considerable sums that the cultivation of the land demands and that occupies the peasants and always provides them with a generous and assured profit. These, according to the concept of M. de Sully, are the true farmers and the true financiers that one must establish and sustain in a kingdom which possesses a great territory; because it is from their riches that must be born the subsistence of the nation, the public ease, the revenues of the sovereign, those of the proprietors, of the clergy, the great sums distributed among all the professions, a numerous population, the strength and the prosperity of the state.

Those who envisage the advantages of a great population only to maintain large armies judge badly the strength of the state. The military esteem men only so far as they are useful to make soldiers; but the statesman regrets the land used to provide the ditch needed to preserve his field. Great armies exhaust the state; a great population and great riches render it redoubtable. The essential advantages that result from a large population are production and consumption which increase or circulate the pecuniary riches of the kingdom. The more a nation with a good territory and active commerce is populated, the richer it is, and the richer it is, the more powerful it is. Today there is perhaps less money wealth in the kingdom than in the past century; but to measure the state of these riches, one must not consider them solely in relation to their quantity, but also in relation to their circulation relative to quantity, to sales and to the favorable price of the products of the kingdom.

ADAM SMITH (1723-1790)

Biographers of Adam Smith (1723-1790) have found little to attract the curious. Born in Scotland, the son of a customs official, educated at Glasgow, then at Balliol College, Oxford, Smith spent most of his mature life as a professor of moral philosophy at the University of Glasgow. Although he traveled widely, he was by temperament and vocation a scholar. If the record is colorless, his one great work, *An Inquiry Into The Nature and Causes of the Wealth of Nations (1776)*, ranks in scope and importance with Newton's *Principia* and places him among intellectual giants of the modern world. By period, he belongs to the second half of the eighteenth century (*The Wealth of Nations* appeared in the same year as the American Declaration of Independence and he died in the second year of the French Revolution). Yet his followers, like those of Karl Marx, regard him as founder and patron saint of one of the two systems of economic thought that dominate our world.

The selections that follow have been taken from the fifth edition of Smith's classic work.

THE WEALTH OF NATIONS

Book I

CHAPTER I

OF THE DIVISION OF LABOUR

The greatest improvement in the productive powers of labour, and the greater part of the skill, dexterity, and judgment with which it is anywhere directed, or applied, seem to have been the effects of the division of labour.

The effects of the division of labour, in the general business of society, will be more easily understood by considering in what manner it operates in some particular manufactures. It is commonly supposed to be carried furthest in some very trifling ones; not perhaps that it really is carried further in them than in others of more importance: but in those trifling manufactures which are destined to supply the small wants of but a small number of people, the whole number of workmen must necessarily be small; and those employed in every different branch of the work can often be collected into the same workhouse, and placed at once under the view of the spectator. In those great manufactures, on the contrary, which are destined to supply the great wants of the great body of the people, every different branch of the work employs so great a number of workmen, that it is impossible to collect them all into the same workhouse. We can seldom see more, at one time, than those employed in one single branch. Though in such manufactures, therefore, the work may really be divided into a much greater number of parts, than in those of a more trifling nature, the division is not near so obvious, and has accordingly been much less observed.

To take an example, therefore, from a very trifling manufacture; but one in which the division of labour has been very often taken notice of, the trade of the pin-maker; a workman not educated to this business (which the division of labour has rendered a distinct trade), nor acquainted with the use of the machinery employed in it (to the invention of which the same division of labour has probably given occasion), could scarce, perhaps, with his utmost industry, make one pin in a day, and certainly could not make twenty. But in the way in which this business is now carried on, not only the whole work is a peculiar trade, but it is divided into a number of branches, of which the greater part are likewise peculiar trades. One man draws out the wire, another straights it, a third cuts it, a fourth points it, a fifth grinds it at the top for receiving the head; to make the head requires two or three distinct operations; to put it on, is a peculiar business, to whiten the pins is another; it is even a trade by itself to put them into the paper; and the important business of making a pin is, in this manner, divided into about eighteen distinct operations, which, in some manufactories, are all performed by distinct hands, though in others the same man will sometimes perform two or three of them. I have seen a small manufactory of this kind where ten men only were employed, and where some of them consequently performed two or three distinct operations. But though they were very poor, and therefore but indifferently accommodated with the necessary machinery, they could, when they exerted themselves, make among them about twelve pounds of pins in a day. There are in a pound upwards of four thousand pins of a middling size. Those ten persons, therefore, could make among them upwards of forty-eight thousand pins in a day. Each person, therefore, making a tenth part of forty-eight thousand pins, might be considered as making four thousand eight hundred pins in a day. But if they had all wrought separately and independently, and without any of them having been educated to this peculiar business, they certainly could not each of them have made twenty, perhaps not one pin in a day; that is, certainly, not the two hundred and fortieth, perhaps not the four thousand eight hundredth part of what they are at present capable of performing, in consequence of a proper division and combination of their different operations.

In every other art and manufacture, the effects of the division of labour are similar to what they are in this very trifling one; though, in many of them, the labour can neither be so much subdivided, nor reduced to so great a simplicity of operation. The division of labour, however, so far as it can be introduced, occasions, in every art, a proportionable increase of the productive powers of labour. The separation of different trades and employments from one another, seems to have taken place, in consequence of this advantage. This separation too is generally carried furthest in those countries which enjoy the highest degree of industry and improvement; what is the work of one man in a rude state of society, being generally that of several in an improved one. In every improved society, the farmer is generally nothing but a farmer; the manufacturer nothing but a manufacturer. The labour, too, which is necessary to produce any one complete manufacture, is almost always divided among a great number of hands. How many different trades are employed in each branch of the linen and woolen manufactures, from the growers of the flax and the wool, to the bleachers and smoothers of the linen, or to the dyers and dressers of the cloth! The nature of agriculture, indeed, does not admit of so many subdivisions of labour, nor of so complete a separation of one business from another, as manufactures. It is impossible to separate so entirely the business of the grazier from that of the corn-farmer, as the trade of the carpenter is commonly separated from that of the smith. The spinner is almost always a distinct person from the weaver; but the plowman, the harrower, the sower of the seed, and the reaper of the corn, are often the same. The occasions for those different sorts of labour returning with the different seasons of the year, it is impossible that one man should be constantly employed in any one of them. This impossibility of making so complete and entire a separation of all the different branches of labour employed in agriculture, is perhaps the reason why the improvement of the productive powers of labour in this art, does not always keep pace with their improvement in manufactures. The most opulent nations, indeed, generally excel all their neighbors in agriculture as well as in manufactures; but they are commonly more distinguished by their superiority in the latter than in the former. . . . The corn of Poland, in the same degree of goodness, is as cheap as that of France, notwithstanding the superior opulence and improvement of the latter country. But though the poor country, notwithstanding the inferiority of its cultivation, can, in some measure, rival the rich in the cheapness and goodness of its corn, it can pretend to no such competition in its manufactures; at least if those manufactures suit the soil, climate and situation of the rich country. . . . In Poland there are said to be scarce any manufactures of any kind, a few of those coarser household manufactures excepted, without which no country can well subsist.

This great increase of the quantity of work, which, in consequence of the division of labour, the same number of people are capable of performing, is owing to three different circumstances; first to the increase of dexterity in every particular workman; secondly, to the saving of the time which is commonly lost in passing from one species of work to another; and lastly, to the invention of a great number of machines which facilitate and abridge labour, and enable one man to do the work of many.

First, the improvement of the dexterity of the workman necessarily increases the quantity of the work he can perform; and the division of labour, by reducing every man's business to some one simple operation, and by making this operation the sole employment of his life, necessarily increases very much the dexterity of the workman. . . .

Secondly, the advantage which is gained by saving the time commonly lost in passing from one sort of work to another, is much greater than we should at first view be apt to imagine it. It is impossible to pass very quickly from one kind of work to another, that is carried on in a different place, and with quite different tools. A country weaver, who cultivates a small farm, must lose a good deal of time in passing from his loom to the field, and from the field to his loom. When the two trades can be carried on in the same workhouse, the loss of time is no doubt much less. It is even in this case, however, very considerable. A man commonly saunters a little in turning his hand from one sort of employment to another. When he first begins the new work he is seldom very keen and hearty; his mind, as they say, does not go to it, and for some time he rather trifles than applies to good purpose. The habit of sauntering and of indolent, careless application, which is naturally, or rather necessarily, acquired by every country workman who is obliged to change his work and his tools every half hour and to apply his hand in twenty different ways almost every day of his life, renders him almost always slothful and lazy and incapable of any vigorous application even on the most pressing occasions. Independent, therefore, of his deficiency in point of dexterity, this cause alone must always reduce considerably the quantity of work which he is capable of performing.

Thirdly, and lastly, every body must be sensible how much labour is facilitated and abridged by the application of proper machinery. It is unnecessary to give any example. I shall only observe, therefore, that the invention of all those machines by which labour is so much facilitated and abridged, seems to have been originally owing to the division of labour. Men are much more likely to discover easier and readier methods of attaining any object, when the whole attention of their minds is directed towards that single object, than when it is dissipated among a great variety of things. But in consequence of the division of labour, the whole of every man's attention comes naturally to be directed towards some one very simple object. It is naturally to be expected, therefore, that some one or other of those who are employed in each particular branch of labour should soon find out easier and readier methods of performing their own particular work, wherever the nature of it admits of such improvement.

All the improvements in machinery, however, have by no means been the inventions of those who had occasion to use the machines. Many improvements have been made by the ingenuity of the makers of the machines, when to make them became the business of a peculiar trade; and some by that of those who are called philosophers or men of speculation, whose trade it is not to do anything, but to observe everything; and who, upon that account, are often capable of combining together the powers of the most distant and dissimilar objects. In the progress of society, philosophy or speculation becomes, like every other employment, the principal or sole trade and occupation of a particular class of citizens. . . .

It is the great multiplication of the productions of all the different arts, in consequence of the division of labour, which occasions, in a well-governed society, that universal opulence which extends itself to the lowest ranks of the people. Every workman has a great quantity of his own work to dispose of beyond what he himself has occasion for; and every other workman being exactly in the same situation, he is enabled to exchange a great quantity of his own goods for a great quantity, or, what comes to the same thing, for the price of a great quantity of theirs. He supplies them abundantly with what they have occasion for, and they accommodate him as amply with what he has occasion for, and a general plenty diffuses itself through all the different ranks of the society.

Observe the accommodation of the most common artificer or day-labourer in a civilized and thriving country, and you will perceive that the number of people of whose industry a part, though but a small part, has been employed in procuring him this accommodation, exceeds all computation. . . . Compared, indeed, with the more extravagant luxury of the great, his accommodation must no doubt appear extremely simple and easy; and yet it may be true, perhaps, that the accommodation of an European prince does not always so much exceed that of an industrious and frugal peasant, as the accommodation of the latter exceeds that of many an African king, the absolute master of the lives and liberties of ten thousand naked savages.

CHAPTER II

OF THE PRINCIPLE WHICH GIVES OCCASION

TO THE DIVISION OF LABOUR

This division of labour, from which so many advantages are derived, is not originally the effect of any human wisdom, which foresees and intends that general opulence to which it gives occasion. It is the necessary, though very slow and gradual, consequence of a certain propensity in human nature which has in view no such extensive utility; the propensity to truck, barter, and exchange one thing for another.

Whether this propensity be one of those original principles in human nature, of which no further account can be given; or whether, as seems more probable, it be the necessary consequence of the faculties of reason and speech, it belongs not to our present subject to enquire. It is common to all men, and to be found in no other race of animals, which seem to know neither this nor any other species of contracts. . . . In almost every other race of animals each individual, when it is grown up to maturity, is entirely independent, and in its natural state has occasion for the assistance of no other living creature. But man has an almost constant occasion for the help of his brethren, and it is in vain for him to expect it from their benevolence only. He will be more likely to prevail if he can interest their self-love in his favour, and show them that it is for their own advantage to do for him what he requires of them. Whoever offers to another a bargain of any kind, proposes to do this. Give me that which I want, and you shall have this which you want, is the meaning of every such offer; and it is in this manner that we obtain from one another the far greater part of those good offices which we stand in need of. It is not from the benevolence of the butcher, the brewer, or the baker, that we expect our dinner, but from their regard for their own interest. We address ourselves, not to their humanity but to their self-love, and never talk to them of our own necessities but of their advantages. Nobody but a beggar chuses to depend chiefly upon the benevolence of his fellow-citizens. . . .

The difference of natural talents in different men is, in reality, much less than we are aware of; and the very different genius which appears to distinguish men of different professions, when grown up to maturity, is not upon many occasions so much the cause, as the effect of the division of labour. The difference between the most dissimilar characters, between a philosopher and a common street porter, for example, seems to arise not so much from nature, as from habit, custom, and education. . . .

CHAPTER III

THAT THE DIVISION OF LABOUR IS LIMITED

BY THE EXTENT OF THE MARKET

As it is the power of exchanging that gives occasion to the division of labour, so the extent of this division must always be limited by the extent of that power, or, in other words, by the extent of the market. When the market is very small, no person can have any encouragement to dedicate himself entirely to one employment, for want of the power to exchange all that surplus part of the produce of his own labour, which is over and above

man needs man

man: the same from street porter → philosopher

his own consumption, for such parts of the produce of other men's labour as he has occasion for.

CHAPTER V

OF THE REAL AND NOMINAL PRICE OF COMMODITIES, OR OF THEIR PRICE IN LABOUR, AND THEIR PRICE IN MONEY

Every man is rich or poor according to the degree in which he can afford to enjoy the necessaries, conveniences, and amusements of human life. But after the division of labour has once thoroughly taken place, it is but a very small part of these with which a man's own labour can supply him. The far greater part of them he must derive from the labour of other people, and he must be rich or poor according to the quantity of that labour which he can command, or which he can afford to purchase. The value of any commodity, therefore, to the person who possesses it, and who means not to use or consume it himself, but to exchange it for other commodities, is equal to the quantity of labour which it enables him to purchase or command. Labour, therefore, is the real measure of the exchangeable value of all commodities.

But though equal quantities of labour are always of equal value to the labourer, yet to the person who employs him they appear sometimes to be of greater and sometimes of smaller value. He purchases them sometimes with a greater and sometimes with a smaller quantity of goods, and to him the price of labour seems to vary like that of all other things. It appears to him dear in the one case, and cheap in the other. In reality, however, it is the goods which are cheap in the one case, and dear in the other.

In this popular sense, therefore, labour, like commodities, may be said to have a real and a nominal price. Its real price may be said to consist in the quantity of the necessaries and conveniences of life which are given for it; its nominal price, in the quantity of money. The labourer is rich or poor, is well or ill rewarded, in proportion to the real, not to the nominal price of his labour.

CHAPTER VI

OF THE COMPONENT PARTS OF THE PRICE OF COMMODITIES

In that early and rude state of society which precedes both the accumulation of stock and the appropriation of land, the proportion between the quantities of labour necessary for acquiring different objects seems to be the only circumstance which can afford any rule for exchanging them for one another. . . .

As soon as stock has accumulated in the hands of particular persons, some of them will naturally employ it in setting to work industrious people, whom they will supply with materials and subsistence, in order to make a profit by the sale of their work, or by what their labour adds to the value of the material. In exchanging the complete manufacture either for money, for labour, or for other goods, over and above what may be sufficient to pay the price of the materials, and the wages of the workmen, something must be given for the profits of the undertaker of the work who hazards his stock in this adventure. . . . He could have no interest to employ them, unless he expected from the sale of their work something more than what was sufficient to replace his stock to him; and he could have no interest to employ a great stock rather than a small one, unless his profits were to bear some proportion to the extent of his stock. . . .

As soon as the land of any country has all become private property, the landlords, like all other men, love to reap where they never sowed, and demand a rent even for its natural produce. The wood of the forest, the grass of the field, and all the natural fruits of the earth, which, when land was common, cost the labourer only the trouble of gathering them, come, even to him, to have an additional price fixed upon them. He must give up to the landlord a portion of what his labour either collects or produces. This portion, or what comes to the same thing, the price of this portion, constitutes the rent of the land, and in the price of the greater part of commodities makes a third component part.

The real value of all the different component parts of price, it must be observed, is measured by the quantity of labour which they can, each of them, purchase or command. Labour measures the value not only of that part of price which resolves itself into labour, but of that which resolves itself into rent, and of that which resolves itself into profit.

In every society the price of every commodity finally resolves itself into some one or other, or all of those three parts; and in every improved society, all the three enter more or less, as component parts, into the price of the far greater part of commodities.

In the price of corn, for example, one part pays the rent of the landlord, another pays the wages or maintenance of the labourers and labouring cattle employed in producing it, and the third pays the profit of the farmer. . . .

As any particular commodity comes to be more manufactured, that part of the price which resolves itself into wages and profit, comes to be greater in proportion to that which resolves itself into rent. In the progress of the manufacture, not only the number of profits increase, but every subsequent profit is greater than the foregoing; because the capital which employes the weavers, for example, must be greater than that which employs the spinners; because it not only replaces that capital with its profits, but pays, besides, the wages of the weavers; and the profits must always bear some proportion to the capital. . . .

CHAPTER VIII

OF THE WAGES OF LABOUR

The produce of labour constitutes the natural recompence or wages of labour.

In that original state of things, which precedes both the appropriation of land and the accumulation of stock, the whole produce of labour belongs to the labourer. He has neither landlord nor master to share with him. . . .

As soon as land becomes private property, the landlord demands a share of almost all the produce which the labourer can either raise, or collect from it. His rent makes the first deduction from the produce of the labour which is employed upon the land.

It seldom happens that the person who tills the ground has wherewithal to maintain himself till he reaps the harvest. His maintenance is generally advanced to him from the stock of a master, the farmer who employs him, and who would have no interest to employ him, unless he was to share in the produce of his labour, or unless his stock was to be replaced to him with a profit. This profit makes a second deduction from the produce of the labour which is employed upon land.

The produce of almost all other labour is liable to the like deduction of profit. In all arts and manufactures the greater part of the workmen stand in need of a master to advance them the materials of their work, and their wages and maintenance till it be completed. He shares in the produce of their labour, or in the value which it adds to the materials upon which it is bestowed; and in this share consists his profit. . . .

What are the common wages of labour, depends every where upon the contract usually made between those two parties, whose interests are by no means the same. The workmen desire to get as much, the masters to give as little as possible. The former are disposed to combine in order to raise, the latter in order to lower the wages of labour.

It is not, however, difficult to foresee which of the two parties must, upon all ordinary occasions, have the advantage in the dispute, and force the other into a compliance with their terms. The masters, being fewer in number, can combine much more easily; and the law, besides, authorizes, or at least does not prohibit their combinations, while it prohibits those of the workmen. We have no acts of Parliament against combining to lower the price of work; but many against combining to raise it. In all such disputes the masters can hold out much longer. A landlord, a farmer, a master manufacturer, or merchant, though they did not employ a single workman, could generally live a year or two upon the stocks which they have already acquired. Many workmen could not subsist a week, few could subsist a month, and scarce any a year without employment. In the long run the workman may be as necessary to his master as his master is to him; but the necessity is not so immediate.

We rarely hear, it has been said, of the combinations of masters; though frequently of those of workmen. But whoever imagines, upon this account, that masters rarely combine, is as ignorant of the world as of the subject. Masters are always and everywhere in a sort of tacit, but constant and uniform, combination, not to raise the wages of labour above their actual rate. To violate this combination is everywhere a most unpopular action, and a sort of reproach to a master among his neighbors and equals. We seldom, indeed, hear of this combination, because it is the usual, and one may say, the natural state of things which nobody ever hears of. Masters, too, sometimes enter into particular combinations to sink the wages of labour even below this rate. These are always conducted with the utmost silence and secrecy, till the moment of execution, and when the workmen yield, as they sometimes do, without resistance, though severely felt by them, they are never heard of by other people. Such combinations, however, are frequently resisted by a contrary defensive combination of the workmen; who sometimes, too, without any provocation of this kind, combine of their own accord to raise the price of their labour. Their usual pretences are, sometimes the high price of provisions; sometimes the great profit which their masters make by their work. But whether their combinations be offensive or defensive, they are always abundantly heard of. In order to bring the point to a speedy decision, they have always recourse to the loudest clamour, and sometimes to the most shocking violence and outrage. They are desperate, and act with the folly and extravagance of desperate men, who must either starve, or frighten their masters into an immediate compliance with their demands. The masters upon these occasions are just as clamourous upon the other side, and never cease to call aloud for the assistance of the civil magistrate, and the rigorous execution of those laws which have been enacted with so much severity against the combinations of servants, labourers, and journeymen. The workmen, accordingly, very seldom derive any advantage from the violence of those tumultuous combinations, which, partly from the interposition of the civil magistrate, partly from the superior steadiness of the masters, partly from the necessity which the greater part of the workmen are under of submitting for the sake of present subsistence, generally end in nothing, but the punishment or ruin of the ring-leaders.

But though in disputes with their workmen, masters must generally have the advantage, there is however a certain rate below which it seems impossible to reduce, for any considerable time, the ordinary wages even of the lowest species of labour.

A man must always live by his work, and his wages must at least be sufficient to maintain him. They must even upon most occasions be somewhat more; otherwise it would be impossible for him to bring up a family, and the race of such workmen could not last beyond the first generation. . . . There are certain circumstances, however, which sometimes give the labourers an advantage, and enable them to raise their wages considerably above this rate; evidently the lowest which is consistent with common humanity.

When in any country the demand for those who live by wages, labourers, journeymen, servants of every kind, is continually increasing; when every year furnishes employment for a greater number than had been employed the year before, the workmen have no occasion to combine in order to raise their wages. The scarcity of hands occasions a competition among masters, who bid against one another, in order to get workmen, and thus voluntarily break through the natural combination of masters not to raise wages.

The demand for those who live by wages, it is evident, cannot increase but in proportion to the increase of the funds which are destined for the payment of wages. . . .

The demand for those who live by wages, therefore, necessarily increases with the increase of the revenue and stock of every country, and cannot possibly increase without it. The increase of revenue and stock is the increase of national wealth. The demand for those who live by wages, therefore, naturally increases with the increase of national wealth, and cannot possibly increase without it.

It is not the actual greatness of national wealth, but its continual increase, which occasions a rise in the wages of labour. It is not, accordingly, in the richest countries, but in the most thriving, or in those which are growing rich the fastest, that the wages of labour are highest. . . .

The real compense of labour, the real quantity of the necessaries and conveniences of life which it can procure to the labourer, has, during the course of the present century, increased perhaps in a still greater proportion than its money price. Not only grain has become somewhat cheaper, but many other things, from which the industrious poor derive an agreeable and wholesome variety of food, have become a great deal cheaper. . . .

Is this improvement in the circumstances of the lower ranks of the people to be regarded as an advantage or as an inconvenience to the society? The answer seems at first sight abundantly plain. Servants, labourers and workmen of different kinds make up the far greater part of every great political society. But what improves the circumstances of the greater part can never be regarded as an inconvenience to the whole. No society can surely be flourishing and happy, of which the far greater part of the members are poor and miserable. It is but equity, besides, that they who feed, clothe and lodge the whole body of the people should have such a share of the produce of their own labour as to be themselves tolerably well fed, clothed and lodged. . . .

Every species of animals naturally multiplies in proportion

to the means of their subsistence, and no species can ever multiply beyond it. But in civilized society it is only among the inferior ranks of people that the scantiness of subsistence can set limits to the further multiplication of the human species; and it can do so in no other way than by destroying a great part of the children which their fruitful marriages produce.

The liberal reward of labour, by enabling them to provide better for their children, and consequently to bring up a greater number, naturally tends to widen and extend those limits. It deserves to be remarked, too, that it necessarily does this as nearly as possible in the proportion which the demand for labour requires. If this demand is continually increasing, the reward of labour must necessarily encourage in such a manner the marriage and multiplication of labourers, as may enable them to supply that continually increasing demand by a continually increasing population. If the reward should at any time be less than what was requisite for this purpose, the deficiency of hands would soon raise it; and if it should at any time be more, their excessive multiplication would soon lower it to this necessary rate. The market would be so much understocked with labour in the one case, and so much overstocked in the other, as would soon force back its price to that proper rate which the circumstances of the society required. It is in this manner that the demand for men, like that for any other commodity, necessarily regulates the production of men; quickens it when it goes on too slowly, and stops it when it advances too fast. . . .

The liberal reward of labour, as it encourages the propagation, so it increases the industry of the common people. The wages of labour are the encouragement of industry, which, like every other human quality, improves in proportion to the encouragement it receives. A plentiful subsistence increases the bodily strength of the labourer, and the comfortable hope of bettering his condition, and of ending his days perhaps in ease and plenty, animates him to exert that strength to the utmost. Where wages are high, accordingly, we shall always find the workmen more active, diligent, and expeditious than where they are low: in England, for example, than in Scotland; in the neighbourhood of great towns than in remote country places. Some workmen, indeed, when they can earn in four days what will maintain them through the week, will be idle the other three. This, however, is by no means the case with the greater part. Workmen, on the contrary, when they are liberally paid by the piece, are very apt to over-work themselves, and to ruin their health and constitution in a few years. . . Excessive application during four days of the week is frequently the real cause of the idleness of the other three, so much and so loudly complained of. Great labour either of mind or body, continued for several days together, is in most men naturally followed by a great desire of relaxation, which, if not restrained by force or by some strong necessity, is almost irresistible. It is the call of nature, which requires to be relieved by some indulgence, sometimes of ease only, but sometimes, too, of dissipation and diversion. If it is not complied with, the consequences are often dangerous, and sometimes fatal, and such as almost always, sooner or later, bring on the peculiar infirmity of the trade. If masters would always listen to the dictates of reason and humanity, they have frequently occasion rather to moderate than to animate the application of many of their workmen. It will be found, I believe, in every sort of trade, that the man who works so moderately as to be able to work constantly, not only preserves his health the longest, but, in the course of the year, executes the greatest quantity of work. . . .

Book IV

CHAPTER I

OF THE PRINCIPLES OF THE COMMERCIAL OR MERCANTILE

SYSTEM

That wealth consists in money, or in gold and silver, is a popular notion which naturally arises from the double function of money, as the instrument of commerce, and as the measure of value. In consequence of its being the instrument of commerce, when we have money we can more readily obtain whatever else we have occasion for, than by means of any other commodity. The great affair we always find is to get money. . . .

A rich country, in the same manner as a rich man, is supposed to be a country abounding in money; and to heap up gold and silver in any country is supposed to be the readiest way to enrich it. For some time after the discovery of America, the first enquiry of the Spaniards, when they arrived upon any unknown coast, used to be, if there was any gold or silver to be found in the neighborhood? By the information which they received, they judged whether it was worth while to make a settlement there, or if the country was worth the conquering. . . .

In consequence of these popular notions, all the different nations of Europe have studied, though to little purpose, every possible means of accumulating gold and silver in their respective countries. Spain and Portugal, the proprietors of the principal mines which supply Europe with those metals, have either prohibited their exportation under the severest penalties, or subjected it to a considerable duty. The like prohibition seems anciently to have been made a part of the policy of most other European nations. It is even to be found, where we should least of all expect to find it, in some old Scotch acts of parliament, which forbid under heavy penalties the carrying of gold or silver *forth from the kingdom.* The like policy anciently took place both in France and England.

When those countries became commercial, the merchants found this prohibition, upon many occasions, extremely inconvenient. They could frequently buy more advantageously with gold or silver than with any other commodity, the foreign goods which they wanted, either to import into their own, or to carry to some other foreign country. They remonstrated, therefore, against this prohibition as hurtful to trade. . . .

It would be too ridiculous to go about seriously to prove, that wealth does not consist in money, or in gold and silver; but in what money purchases, and is valuable only for purchasing. Money, no doubt, makes always a part of the national capital; but it has already been shown that it generally makes but a small part, and always the most unprofitable part of it. . . .

The two principles being established, however, that wealth consisted in gold and silver, and that those metals could be brought into a country which had no mines only by the balance of trade, or by exporting to a greater value than it imported; it necessarily became the great object of political economy to diminish as much as possible the importation of foreign goods for home consumption, and to increase as much as possible the exportation of the produce of domestic industry. Its two great engines for enriching the country, therefore, were restraints upon importation, and encouragements to exportation.

The restraints upon importation were of two kinds.

First, Restraints upon the importation of such foreign goods for home consumption as could be produced at home, from whatever country they were imported.

Secondly, Restraints upon the importation of goods of almost all kinds from those particular countries with which the balance of trade was supposed to be disadvantageous.

Those different restraints consisted sometimes in high duties, and sometimes in absolute prohibitions. . . .

Chapter II

OF RESTRAINTS UPON THE IMPORTATION FROM FOREIGN COUNTRIES OF SUCH GOODS AS CAN BE PRODUCED AT HOME

By restraining, either by high duties, or by absolute prohibitions, the importation of such goods from foreign countries as can be produced at home, the monopoly of the home market is more or less secured to the domestic industry employed in producing them. . . .

That this monopoly of the home market frequently gives great encouragement to that particular species of industry which enjoys it, and frequently turns toward that employment a greater share of both the labour and stock of the society than would otherwise have gone to it, cannot be doubted. But whether it tends either to increase the general industry of the society, or to give it the most advantageous direction, is not, perhaps, altogether so evident.

The general industry of the society never can exceed what the capital of the society can employ. As the number of workmen that can be kept in employment by any particular person must bear a certain proportion to his capital, so the number of those that can be continually employed by all the members of a great society must bear a certain proportion to the whole capital of that society, and never can exceed that proportion. No regulation of commerce can increase the quantity of industry in any society beyond what its capital can maintain. It can only divert a part of it into a direction into which it might not otherwise have gone; and it is by no means certain that this artificial direction is likely to be more advantageous to the society than that into which it would have gone of its own accord.

Every individual is continually exerting himself to find out the most advantageous employment for whatever capital he can command. It is his own advantage, indeed, and not that of the society which he has in view. But the study of his own advantage naturally, or rather necessarily leads him to prefer that employment which is most advantageous to the society.

First, every individual endeavors to employ his capital as near home as he can, and consequently as much as he can in the support of domestic industry; provided always that he can thereby obtain the ordinary, or not a great deal less than the ordinary profits of stock.

Thus, upon equal or nearly equal profits, every wholesale merchant naturally prefers the home trade to the foreign trade of consumption, and the foreign trade of consumption to the carrying trade. In the home trade his capital is never so long out of his sight as it frequently is in the foreign trade of consumption. He can know better the character and situation of the persons whom he trusts, and if he should happen to be deceived, he knows better the laws of the country from which he must seek redress. . .

Secondly, every individual who employs his capital in the support of domestic industry, necessarily endeavors so to direct that industry that its produce may be of the greatest possible value.

The produce of industry is what it adds to the subject or materials upon which it is employed. In proportion as the value of this produce is great or small, so will likewise be the profits of the employer. But it is only for the sake of profit that any man employs a capital in the support of industry; and he will always, therefore, endeavor to employ it in the support of that industry of which the produce is likely to be of the greatest value, or to exchange for the greatest quantity either of money or of other goods.

But the annual revenue of every society is always precisely equal to the exchangeable value of the whole annual produce of its industry, or rather is precisely the same thing with that exchangeable value. As every individual, therefore, endeavors as much as he can both to employ his capital in the support of domestic industry, and so to direct that industry that its produce may be of the greatest value; every individual necessarily labours to render the annual revenue of the society as great as he can. He generally, indeed, neither intends to promote the public interest, nor knows how much he is promoting it. By preferring the support of domestic to that of foreign industry, he intends only his own security; and by directing that industry in such a manner as its produce may be of the greatest value, he intends only his own gain, and he is in this, as in many other cases, led by an invisible hand to promote an end which was no part of his intention. Nor is it always the worse for the society that it was no part of it. By pursuing his own interest he frequently promotes that of the society more effectually than when he really intends to promote it. I have never known much good done by those who affected to trade for the public good. It is an affectation, indeed, not very common among merchants, and very few words need be employed in dissuading them from it.

What is the species of domestic industry which his capital can employ, and of which the produce is likely to be of the greatest value, every individual, it is evident, can, in his local situation, judge much better than any statesman or lawgiver can do for him. The statesman who should attempt to direct private people in what manner they ought to employ their capitals, would not only load himself with a most unnecessary attention, but assume an authority which could safely be trusted, not only to no single person, but to no council or senate whatever, and which would nowhere be so dangerous as in the hands of a man who had folly and presumption enough to fancy himself fit to exercise it.

To give the monopoly of the home market to the produce of domestic industry, in any particular art or manufacture, is in some measure to direct private people in what manner they ought to employ their capitals, and must, in almost all cases, be either a useless or a hurtful regulation. If the produce of domestic can be brought there as cheap as that of foreign industry, the regulation is evidently useless. If it cannot, it must generally be hurtful. It is the maxim of every prudent master of a family, never to attempt to make at home what it will cost him more to make than to buy. The tailor does not attempt to make his own shoes, but buys them of the shoemaker. The shoemaker does not attempt to make his own clothes, but employs a tailor. The farmer attempts to make neither the one nor the other, but employs those different artificers. All of them find it to their interest to employ their whole industry in a way in which they have some advantage over their neighbours, and to purchase with a part of its produce, or what is the same thing, with the price of a part of it, whatever else they have occasion for.

What is prudence in the conduct of every private family can scarce be folly in that of a great kingdom. If a foreign country can supply us with a commodity cheaper than we ourselves can make it, better buy it of them with some part of the produce of our own industry employed in a way in which we have some advantage. The general industry of the country, being always in proportion to the capital which employes it, will not thereby be diminished, no more than that of the above-mentioned artificers; but only left to find out the way in which it can be employed with the greatest advantage. It is certainly not employed to the greatest advantage when it is thus directed towards an object which it can buy cheaper than it can make. The value of its annual produce is certainly more or less diminished when it is thus turned away from producing commodities evidently of more value than the commodity which it is directed to produce. According to the supposition, that commodity could be purchased from foreign countries cheaper than it can be made at home. It could, therefore, have been purchased with a part only of the commodities, or, what is the same thing, with a part only of the price of the commodities, which the industry employed by an equal capital would have produced at home, had it been left to follow its natural course. The industry of the country, therefore, is thus turned away from a more to a less advantageous employment, and the exchangeable value of its annual produce, instead of being increased, according to the intention of the lawgiver, must necessarily be diminished by every such regulation. . . .

The natural advantages which one country has over another in producing particular commodities are sometimes so great, that it is acknowledged by all the world to be in vain to struggle with them. By means of glasses, hotbeds, and hotwalls, very good grapes can be raised in Scotland, and very good wine too can be made of them at about thirty times the expense for which at least equally good can be brought from foreign countries. Would it be a reasonable law to prohibit the importation of all foreign wines, merely to encourage the making of claret and burgundy in Scotland? . . .

Chapter IX

OF THE AGRICULTURAL SYSTEMS, OR OF THOSE SYSTEMS OF
POLITICAL ECONOMY, WHICH REPRESENT THE PRODUCE OF
LAND AS EITHER THE SOLE OR THE PRINCIPAL SOURCE OF
THE REVENUE AND WEALTH OF EVERY COUNTRY

That system which represents the produce of land as the
sole source of the revenue and wealth of every country has, so
far as I know, never been adopted by any nation, and it at
present exists only in the speculations of a few great men of
learning and ingenuity in France. It would not, surely, be worth
while to examine at great length the errors of a system which
has never done, and probably never will do any harm in any
part of the world. . . .

If the rod be bent too much one way, says the proverb, in
order to make it straight you must bend it as much the other.
The French philosophers, who have proposed the system which
represents agriculture as the sole source of revenue and wealth
of every country, seem to have adopted this proverbial maxim;
and as in the plan of Mr. Colbert the industry of the towns was
certainly over-valued in comparison with that of the country; so
in their system it seems to be as certainly under-valued.

The different orders of people who have ever been supposed
to contribute in any respect towards the annual produce of the
land and labour of the country, they divide into three classes.
The first is the class of the proprietors of land. The second is
the class of the cultivators, of farmers and country labourers,
whom they honour with the peculiar appellation of the productive class. The third is the class of artificers, manufacturers and
merchants, whom they endeavour to degrade by the humiliating
appellation of the barren or unproductive class. . . .

The unproductive class, that of merchants, artificers and
manufacturers, is maintained and employed altogether at the
expense of the two other classes, of that of proprietors, and of
that of cultivators. They furnish it both with the materials of its
work and with the funds of its subsistence, with the corn and
cattle which it consumes while it is employed about that work.
The proprietors and cultivators finally pay both the wages of all
workmen of the unproductive class, and the profits of all their
employers. Those workmen and their employers are properly the

servants of the proprietors and cultivators. They are only servants who work without doors, as menial servants work within. Both the one and the other, however, are equally maintained at the expense of the same masters. The labour of both is equally unproductive. It adds nothing to the value of the sum total of the rude produce of the land. Instead of increasing the value of the sum total, it is a charge and expense which must be paid out of it. . . .

. . . The following observations may serve to show the impropriety of this representation. . . .

. . . The annual produce of the land and labour of any society can be augmented only in two ways; either, first, by some improvement in the productive powers of the useful labour actually maintained within it; or, secondly, by some increase in the quantity of that labour.

The improvement in the productive powers of useful labour depends, first, upon the improvement in the ability of the workman; and, secondly, upon that of the machinery with which he works. But the labour of the artificers and manufacturers, as it is capable of being subdivided, and the labour of each workman reduced to a greater simplicity of operation, than that of farmers and country labourers, so it is likewise capable of both of these sorts of improvement in a much higher degree. In this respect, therefore, the class of cultivators can have no sort of advantage over that of artificers and manufacturers.

The increase in the quantity of useful labour actually employed within any society, must depend altogether upon the increase of the capital which employs it; and the increase of that capital again must be exactly equal to the amount of the savings from the revenue, either of the particular persons who manage and direct the employment of that capital, or of some other persons who lend it to them. If merchants, artificers and manufacturers are, as this system seems to suppose, naturally more inclined to parsimony and saving than proprietors and cultivators, they are, so far, more likely to augment the quantity of useful labour employed within their society, and consequently to increase its real revenue, the annual produce of its land and labour. . . .

This system, however, with all its imperfections, is, perhaps, the nearest approximation to the truth that has yet been published upon the subject of political economy, and is upon that account well worth the consideration of every man who wishes to examine with attention the principles of that very important science. Though in representing the labour which is employed upon land as the only productive labour, the notions which it inculcates are perhaps too narrow and confined; yet in representing the wealth of nations as consisting, not in the unconsumable riches of money, but in the consumable goods annually reproduced by the labour of the society; and in representing perfect liberty as the only effectual expedient for rendering this annual reproduction the greatest possible, its doctrine seems to be in every respect as just as it is generous and liberal. . . .

JEREMY BENTHAM (1748-1832)

The founder of Utilitarianism was a well-to-do, eccentric bachelor who devoted a long life to exposing what he regarded as the archaic, irrational character of English legal and social institutions. The son of a wealthy London barrister, Bentham graduated from Oxford at sixteen and then studied for the law at Lincoln's Inn. He had little use for the "medieval" curriculum at Oxford, even less for English law, which provided the subject for the first of a long series of books and pamphlets. Despite his efforts to apply pure reason and logic to each subject he investigated, Bentham's prose style was abominable and the arguments sometimes almost unintelligible. Fortunately, he attracted a band of able, devoted disciples, including in their number John Stuart Mill, who edited his works for publication and spread his doctrines. Already widely read on the Continent before the French Revolution, his principal influence in England came in the decades following the Napoleonic Wars.

The selections given below are from *The Works of Jeremy Bentham,* Part I, Edinburgh, 1838.

AN INTRODUCTION TO THE PRINCIPLES OF MORALS AND LEGISLATION (1789)

CHAPTER I

OF THE PRINCIPLE OF UTILITY

I. Nature has placed mankind under the governance of two sovereign masters, *pain* and *pleasure*. It is for them alone to point out what we ought to do, as well as to determine what we shall do. On the one hand the standard of right and wrong, on the other the chain of causes and effects, are fastened to their throne. They govern us in all we do, in all we say, in all we think: every effort we can make to throw off our subjection, will serve but to demonstrate and confirm it. In words a man may pretend to abjure their empire: but in reality he will remain subject to it all the while. The *principle of utility* recognises this subjection, and assumes it for the foundation of that system, the object of which is to rear the fabric of felicity by the hands of reason and of law. Systems which attempt to question it, deal in sounds instead of sense, in caprice instead of reason, in darkness instead of light.

But enough of metaphor and declamation: it is not by such means that moral science is to be improved.

II. The principle of utility is the foundation of the present work: it will be proper therefore at the outset to give an explicit and determinate account of what is meant by it. By the principle of utility is meant that principle which approves or disapproves of every action whatsoever, according to the tendency which it appears to have to augment or diminish the happiness of the party whose interest is in question: or, what is the same thing in other words, to promote or to oppose that happiness. I say of every action whatsoever; and therefore not only of every action of a private individual, but of every measure of government.

III.   By utility is meant that property in any object, whereby it tends to produce benefit, advantage, pleasure, good, or happiness, (all this in the present case comes to the same thing) or (what comes again to the same thing)to prevent the happening of mischief, pain, evil, or unhappiness to the party whose interest is considered: if that party be the community in general, then the happiness of the community: if a particular individual, then the happiness of that individual.

IV.   The interest of the community is one of the most general expressions that can occur in the phraseology of morals: no wonder that the meaning of it is often lost. When it has a meaning, it is this. The community is a fictitious *body*, composed of the individual persons who are considered as constituting as it were its *members*. The interest of the community then is, what?—the sum of the interests of the several members who compose it.

V.   It is in vain to talk of the interest of the community, without understanding what is the interest of the individual. A thing is said to promote the interest, or to be *for* the interest, of an individual, when it tends to add to the sum total of his pleasures: or, what comes to the same thing, to diminish the sum total of his pains.

VI.   An action then may be said to be conformable to the principle of utility, or, for shortness sake, to utility, (meaning with respect to the community at large) when the tendency it has to augment the happiness of the community is greater than any it has to diminish it.

VII.   A measure of government (which is but a particular kind of action, performed by a particular person or persons) may be said to be conformable to or dictated by the principle of utility, when in like manner the tendency which it has to augment the happiness of the community is greater than any which it has to diminish it.

VIII. When an action, or in particular a measure of government, is supposed by a man to be conformable to the principle of utility, it may be convenient, for the purposes of discourse, to imagine a kind of law or dictate, called a law or dictate of utility: and to speak of the action in question, as being conformable to such law or dictate.

IX. A man may be said to be a partizan of the principle of utility, when the approbation or disapprobation he annexes to any action, or to any measure, is determined by and proportioned to the tendency which he conceives it to have to augment or to diminish the happiness of the community: or in other words, to its conformity or unconformity to the laws or dictates of utility.

X. Of an action that is conformable to the principle of utility one may always say either that it is one that ought to be done, or at least that it is not one that ought not to be done. One may say also, that it is right it should be done; at least that it is not wrong it should be done: that it is a right action; at least that it is not a wrong action. When thus interpreted, the words ought, and right and wrong, and others of that stamp, have a meaning: when otherwise, they have none.

XI. Has the rectitude of this principle been ever formally contested? It should seem that it had, by those who have not known what they have been meaning. Is it susceptible of any direct proof? It should seem not: for that which is used to prove every thing else, cannot itself be proved: a chain of proofs must have their commencement somewhere. To give such proof is as impossible as it is needless.

XII. Not that there is or ever has been that human creature breathing, however stupid or perverse, who has not on many, perhaps on most occasions of his life, deferred to it. By the natural constitution of the human frame, on most occasions of their lives men in general embrace this principle, without thinking of it: if not for the ordering of their own actions, yet for the trying of their own actions, as well as of those of other men. There have been, at the same time, not many, perhaps, even of the most intelligent, who have been disposed to embrace it purely and without reserve. There are even few who have not taken some occasion or other to quarrel with it, either on account of their not understanding always how to apply it, or on account of some prejudice or other which they were afraid to examine into, or could not bear to part with. For such is the stuff that man is made of: in principle and in practice, in a right track and in a wrong one, the rarest of all human qualities is consistency.

XIII. When a man attempts to combat the principle of utility, it is with reasons drawn, without his being aware of it, from that very principle itself. His arguments, if they prove any thing, prove not that the principle is *wrong,* but that, according to the applications he supposes to be made of it, it is *misapplied.* Is it possible for a man to move the earth? Yes; but he must first find out another earth to stand upon. . . .

CHAPTER II

OF PRINCIPLES ADVERSE TO THAT OF UTILITY

I. If the principle of utility be a right principle to be governed by, and that in all cases, it follows from what has been just observed, that whatever principle differs from it in any case must necessarily be a wrong one. To prove any other principle, therefore, to be a wrong one, there needs no more than just to show it to be what it is, a principle of which the dictates are in some point or other different from those of the principle of utility: to state it is to confute it.

II. A principle may be different from that of utility in two ways: 1. By being constantly opposed to it: this is the case with a principle which may be termed the principle of *asceticism.* 2. By being sometimes opposed to it, and sometimes not, as it may happen: this is the case with another, which may be termed the principle of *sympathy* and *antipathy.*

III. By the principle of asceticism I mean that principle, which, like the principle of utility, approves or disapproves of any action, according to the tendency which it appears to have to augment or diminish the happiness of the party whose interest is in question; but in an inverse manner: approving of actions in as far as they tend to diminish his happiness; disapproving of them in as far as they tend to augment it.

IV. It is evident that any one who reprobates any the least particle of pleasure, as such, from whatever source derived, is *pro tanto* a partizan of the principle of asceticism. It is only upon that principle, and not from the principle of utility, that the most abominable pleasure which the vilest of malefactors ever reaped from his crime would be to be reprobated, if it stood alone. The case is, that it never does stand alone; but is necessarily followed by such a quantity of pain (or, what comes to the same thing, such a chance for a certain quantity of pain) that the pleasure in comparison of it, is as nothing: and this is the true and sole, but perfectly sufficient, reason for making it a ground for punishment.

V. There are two classes of men of very different complexions, by whom the principle of asceticism appears to have been embraced; the one a set of moralists, the other a set of religionists. Different accordingly have been the motives which appear to have recommended it to the notice of these different parties. Hope, that is the prospect of pleasure, seems to have animated the former: hope, the aliment of philosophic pride: the hope of honour and reputation at the hands of men. Fear, that is the prospect of pain, the latter: fear, the offspring of superstitious fancy: the fear of future punishment at the hands of a splenetic and revengeful Deity. I say in this case fear: for of the invisible future, fear is more powerful than hope. These circumstances characterize the two different parties among the partizans of the principle of asceticism; the parties and their motives different, the principle the same.

VI. The religious party, however, appear to have carried it farther than the philosophical: they have acted more consistently and less wisely. The philosophical party have scarcely gone farther than to reprobate pleasure: the religious party have frequently gone so far as to make it a matter of merit and of duty to court pain. . . .

VII. From these two sources have flowed the doctrines from which the sentiments of the bulk of mankind have all along received a tincture of this principle; some from the philosophical, some from the religious, some from both. Men of education more frequently from the philosophical, as more suited to the elevation of their sentiments: the vulgar more frequently from the superstitious, as more suited to the narrowness of their intellect, undilated by knowledge: and to the abjectness of their condition, continually open to the attacks of fear. The tinctures, however, derived from the two sources, would naturally intermingle, insomuch that a man would not always know by which of them he was most influenced; and they would often serve to corroborate and enliven one another. It was this conformity that made a kind of alliance between parties of a complexion otherwise so dissimilar: and disposed them to unite upon various occasions against the common enemy, the partizan of the principle of utility, whom they joined in branding with the odious name of Epicurean. . . .

X. The principle of utility is capable of being consistently pursued; and it is but tautology to say, that the more consistently it is pursued, the better it must ever be for humankind. The principle of asceticism never was, nor ever can be, consistently pursued by any living creature. Let but one tenth part of the inhabitants of this earth pursue it consistently, and in a day's time they will have turned it into a hell.

XI. Among principles adverse to that of utility, that which at this day seems to have most influence in matters of government, is what may be called the principle of sympathy and antipathy. By the principle of sympathy and antipathy, I mean that principle which approves or disapproves of certain actions, not on account of their tending to augment the happiness, nor yet on account of their tending to diminish the happiness of the party whose interest is in question, but merely because a man finds himself disposed to approve or disapprove of them: holding up that approbation or disapprobation as a sufficient reason for itself, and disclaiming the necessity of looking out for any extrinsic ground. . . .

XIII. In looking over the catalogue of human actions (says a partizan of this principle) in order to determine which of them are to be marked with the seal of disapprobation, you need but to take counsel of your own feelings: whatever you find in yourself a propensity to condemn, is wrong for that very reason. For the same reason it is also meet for punishment: in what proportion it is adverse to utility, or whether it be adverse to utility at all, is a matter that makes no difference. In that same *proportion* also is it meet for punishment: if you hate much, punish much: if you hate little, punish little: punish as you hate. If you hate not at all, punish not at all: the fine feelings of the soul are not to be overborne and tyrannized by the harsh and rugged dictates of political utility.

XIV. The various systems that have been formed concerning the standard of right and wrong, may all be reduced to the principle of sympathy and antipathy. One account may serve for all of them. They consist all of them in so many contrivances for avoiding the obligation of appealing to any external standard, and for prevailing upon the reader to accept of the author's sentiment or opinion as a reason for itself. The phrases different, but the principle the same.

XV. It is manifest, that the dictates of this principle will frequently coincide with those of utility, though perhaps without intending any such thing. Probably more frequently than not: and hence it is that the business of penal justice is carried on upon that tolerable sort of footing upon which we see it carried on in common at this day. For what more natural or more general ground of hatred to a practice can there be, than the mischievousness of such practice? What all men are exposed to suffer by, all men will be disposed to hate. It is far yet, however, from being a constant ground: for when a man suffers, it is not always that he knows what it is he suffers by. A man may suffer grievously, for instance, by a new tax, without being able to trace up the cause of his sufferings to the injustice of some neighbour, who has eluded the payment of an old one.

XVI. The principle of sympathy and antipathy is most apt to err on the side of severity. It is for applying punishment in most cases which deserve none: in many cases which deserve some, it is for applying more than they deserve. There is no incident imaginable, be it ever so trivial, and so remote from mischief, from which this principle may not extract a ground of punishment. Any difference in taste: any difference in opinion: upon one subject as well as upon another. No disagreement so trifling which perseverance and altercation will not render serious. Each becomes in the other's eyes an enemy, and, if laws permit, a criminal. This is one of the circumstances by which the human race is distinguished (not much indeed to its advantage) from the brute creation.

XVIII. It may be wondered, perhaps, that in all this while no mention has been made of the *theological* principle; meaning that principle which professes to recur for the standard of right and wrong to the will of God. But the case is, this is not in fact a distinct principle. It is never any thing more or less than one or other of the three before-mentioned principles presenting itself under another shape. The will of God here meant cannot be his revealed will, as contained in the sacred writings: for that is a system which nobody ever thinks of recurring to at this time of day, for the details of political administration: and even before it can be applied to the details of private conduct, it is universally allowed, by the most eminent divines of all of persuasions, to stand in need of pretty ample interpretations: else to what use are the works of those divines? And for the guidance of these interpretations, it is also allowed, that some other standard must be assumed. . . . It is plain, therefore, that setting revelation out of the question, no light can ever be thrown upon the standard of right and wrong, by any thing that can be said upon the question, what is God's will. We may be perfectly sure, indeed, that whatever is right is conformable to the will of God; but so far is that from answering the purpose of showing us what is right, that it is necessary to know first whether a thing is right, in order to know from thence whether it be conformable to the will of God. . . .

CHAPTER III

OF THE FOUR SANCTIONS OR SOURCES OF PAIN AND PLEASURE

I. It has been shown that the happiness of the individuals, of whom a community is composed, that is that their pleasures and their security, is the end and the sole end which the legislator ought to have in view: the sole standard, in conformity to which each individual ought, as far as depends upon the legislator, to be *made* to fashion his behaviour. But whether it be this or any thing else that is to be *done,* there is nothing by which a man can ultimately be *made* to do it, but either pain or pleasure. Having taken a general view of these two grand objects (*viz.* pleasure, and what comes to the same thing, immunity from pain) in the character of *final* causes; it will be necessary to take a view of pleasure and pain itself, in the character of *efficient* causes or means.

II. There are four distinguishable sources from which pleasure and pain are in use to flow: considered separately, they may be termed the *physical,* the *political,* the *moral,* and the *religious*: and inasmuch as the pleasures and pains belonging to each of them are capable of giving a binding force to any law or rule of conduct, they may all of them be termed *sanctions*.

III. If it be in the present life, and from the ordinary course of nature, not purposely modified by the interposition of the will of any human being, nor by any extraordinary inter-position of any superior invisible being, that the pleasure or the pain takes place or is expected, it may be said to issue from or to belong to the *physical sanction.*

IV.   If at the hands of a *particular* person or set of per-sons in the community, who under names correspondent to that of *judge,* are chosen for the particular purpose of dispensing it, according to the will of the sovereign or supreme ruling power in the state, it may be said to issue from the *political sanction.*

V.   If at the hands of such *chance* persons in the com-munity, as the party in question may happen in the course of his life to have concerns with, according to each man's spontaneous disposition, and not according to any settled or concerted rule, it may be said to issue from the *moral* or *popular sanction.*

VI.   If from the immediate hand of the superior invisible being, either in the present life, or in a future, it may be said to issue from the *religious sanction.*

VII.   Pleasures or pains which may be expected to issue from the *physical, political,* or *moral* sanctions, must all of them be expected to be experienced, if ever, in the *present* life: those which may be expected to issue from the *religious* sanction, may be expected to be experienced either in the *present* life or *in a future. . . .*

CHAPTER IV

VALUE OF A LOT OF PLEASURE OR PAIN, HOW TO BE MEASURED

I.   Pleasures then, and the avoidance of pains, are the *ends* which the legislator has in view: it behoves him therefore to understand their *value.* Pleasures and pains are the *instruments* he has to work with: it behoves him therefore to understand their force, which is again, in other words, their value.

II.   To a person considered by *himself,* the value of a pleas-ure or pain considered *by itself,* will be greater or less, according to the four following circumstances:

1.   Its *intensity.*
2.   Its *duration.*
3.   Its certainty or *uncertainty.*
4.   Its *propinquity* or *remoteness.*

III.   These are the circumstances which are to be consid-ered in estimating a pleasure or a pain considered each of them by itself. But when the value of any pleasure or pain is considered for the purpose of estimating the tendency of any *act* by which it is produced, there are two other circumstances to be taken into the account; these are,

5. Its *fecundity,* or the chance it has of being followed by sensations of the *same* kind: that is, pleasures, if it be a pleasure: pains, if it be a pain.

6. Its *purity,* or the chance it has of *not* being followed by sensations of the *opposite* kind: that is, pains, if it be a pleasure: pleasures, if it be a pain.

These two last, however, are in strictness scarcely to be deemed properties of the pleasure or the pain itself; they are not, therefore, in strictness to be taken into the account of the value of that pleasure or that pain. They are in strictness to be deemed properties only of the act, or other event, by which such pleasure or pain has been produced; and accordingly are only to be taken into the account of the tendency of such act or such event.

IV. To a *number* of persons, with reference to each of whom the value of a pleasure or a pain is considered, it will be greater or less, according to seven circumstances: to wit, the six preceding ones; viz.:

1. Its *intensity.*
2. Its *duration.*
3. Its *certainty* or *uncertainty.*
4. Its *propinquity* or *remoteness.*
5. Its *fecundity.*
6. Its *purity.*

And one other; to wit:

7. Its *extent;* that is, the number of persons to whom it *extends;* or (in other words) who are affected by it.

V. To take an exact account then of the general tendency of any act, by which the interests of a community are affected, proceed as follows. Begin with any one person of those whose interests seem most immediately to be affected by it: and take an account,

1. Of the value of each distinguishable *pleasure* which appears to be produced by it in the *first* instance.

2. Of the value of each *pain* which appears to be produced by it in the *first* instance.

3. Of the value of each pleasure which appears to be produced by it *after* the first. This constitutes the *fecundity;* of the first *pleasure* and the *impurity* of the first *pain.*

4. Of the value of each *pain* which appears to be produced by it after the first. This constitutes the *fecundity* of the first *pain,* and the *impurity* of the first pleasure.

5. Sum up all the values of all the *pleasures* on the one side, and those of all the pains on the other. The balance, if it be on the side of pleasure, will give the *good* tendency of the act upon the whole, with respect to the interests of that *individual* person; if on the side of pain, the *bad* tendency of it upon the whole.

6. Take an account of the *number* of persons whose interests appear to be concerned; and repeat the above process with respect to each. *Sum up* the numbers expressive of the degrees of *good* tendency, which the act has, with respect to each individual, in regard to whom the tendency of it is *good* upon the whole: do this again with respect to each individual, in regard to whom the tendency of it is *good* upon the whole: do this again with respect to each individual, in regard to whom the tendency of it is *bad* upon the whole. Take the *balance;* which, if on the side of *pleasure,* will give the general *good tendency* of the act, with respect to the total number or community of individuals concerned; if on the side of pain, the general *evil tendency,* with respect to the same community.

VI. It is not to be expected that this process should be strictly pursued previously to every moral judgment, or to every legislative or judicial operation. It may, however, be always kept in view: and as near as the process actually pursued on these occasions approaches to it, so near will such process approach to the character of an exact one.

VII. The same process is alike applicable to pleasure and pain, in whatever shape they appear: and by whatever denomination they are distinguished: to pleasure, whether it be called *good* (which is properly the cause or instrument of pleasure) or *profit* (which is distant pleasure, or the cause or instrument of distant pleasure,) or *convenience,* or *advantage, benefit, emolument, happiness,* and so forth to pain whether it be called *evil,* (which corresponds to *good*) or *mischief, or inconvenience,* or *disadvantage,* or *loss,* or *unhappiness,* and so forth.

VIII.   Nor is this a novel and unwarranted, any more than it is a useless theory. In all this there is nothing but what the practice of mankind, wheresoever they have a clear view of their own interest, is perfectly conformable to. . . .

CHAPTER XV

GENERAL VIEW OF CASES UNMEET FOR PUNISHMENT

I.   The general object which all laws have, or ought to have, in common, is to augment the total happiness of the community; and therefore, in the first place, to exclude, as far as may be, every thing that tends to subtract from that happiness: in other words, to exclude mischief.

II.   But all punishment is mischief: all punishment in itself is evil. Upon the principle of utility, if it ought at all to be admitted, it ought only to be admitted in as far as it promises to exclude some greater evil.

III.   It is plain, therefore, that in the following cases punishment ought not to be inflicted:

1.   Where it is *groundless*: where there is no mischief for it to prevent; the act not being mischievous upon the whole.

2.   Where it must be *inefficacious*: where it cannot act so as to prevent the mischief.

3.   Where it is *unprofitable,* or too *expensive*: where the mischief it would produce would be greater than what it prevented.

4.   Where it is *needless*: where the mischief may be prevented, or cease of itself, without it: that is, at a cheaper rate. . . .

CHAPTER XVI

OF THE PROPORTION BETWEEN PUNISHMENTS AND OFFENSES

I.   We have seen that the general object of all laws is to prevent mischief; that is to say, when it is worth while; but that, where there are no other means of doing this than punishment, there are four cases in which it is *not* worth while.

II.   When it *is* worth while, there are four subordinate designs or objects, which, in the course of his endeavours to compass, as far as may be, that one general object, a legislator, whose views are governed by the principle of utility, comes naturally to propose to himself.

III.   1. His first, most extensive, and most eligible object, is to prevent, in as far as it is possible, and worth while, all sorts of offences whatsoever: in other words, so to manage, that no offence whatsoever may be committed.

IV. 2. But if a man must needs commit an offence of some kind or other, the next object is to induce him to commit an offence *less* mischievous, *rather* than one *more* mischievous: in other words, to choose always the *least* mischievous, of two offences that will either of them suit his purpose.

V. 3. When a man has resolved upon a particular offence, the next object is to dispose him to do *no more* mischief than is *necessary* to his purpose: in other words, to do as little mischief as is consistent with the benefit he has in view.

VI. 4. The last object is, whatever the mischief be, which it is proposed to prevent, to prevent it at as *cheap* a rate as possible.

VII. Subservient to these four objects, or purposes, must be the rules or canons by which the proportion of punishments to offences is to be governed. . . .

TABLE

OF

THE SPRINGS OF ACTION.

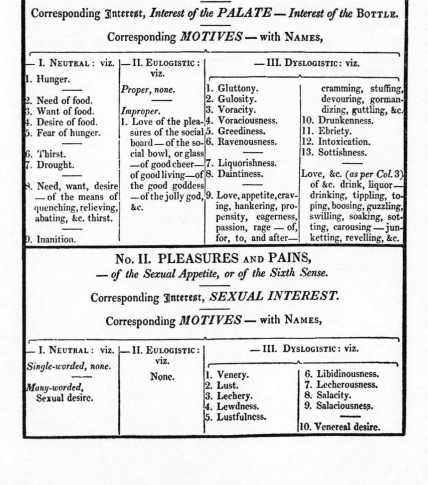

No. I. PLEASURES and PAINS,
— of the Taste *— the* Palate *— the Alimentary Canal — of* Intoxication.

Corresponding Interest, *Interest of the PALATE — Interest of the* Bottle.

Corresponding *MOTIVES* — with Names,

— I. Neutral: viz.	— II. Eulogistic: viz.	— III. Dyslogistic: viz.	
1. Hunger.	*Proper, none.*	1. Gluttony.	cramming, stuffing,
2. Need of food.	*Improper.*	2. Gulosity.	devouring, gorman-
3. Want of food.	1. Love of the plea-	3. Voracity.	dizing, guttling, &c.
4. Desire of food.	sures of the social	4. Voraciousness.	10. Drunkenness.
5. Fear of hunger.	board — of the so-	5. Greediness.	11. Ebriety.
	cial bowl, or glass	6. Ravenousness.	12. Intoxication.
6. Thirst.	—of good cheer—		13. Sottishness.
7. Drought.	of good living—of	7. Liquorishness.	
	the good goddess	8. Daintiness.	Love, &c. (*as per Col.* 3)
8. Need, want, desire	—of the jolly god,		of &c. drink, liquor—
— of the means of	&c.	9. Love, appetite, crav-	drinking, tippling, to-
quenching, relieving,		ing, hankering, pro-	ping, boosing, guzzling,
abating, &c. thirst.		pensity, eagerness,	swilling, soaking, sot-
		passion, rage — of,	ting, carousing — jun-
9. Inanition.		for, to, and after—	ketting, revelling, &c.

No. II. PLEASURES and PAINS,
— of the Sexual Appetite, or of the Sixth Sense.

Corresponding Interest, *SEXUAL INTEREST.*

Corresponding *MOTIVES* — with Names,

— I. Neutral: viz.	— II. Eulogistic: viz.	— III. Dyslogistic: viz.	
Single-worded, none.	None.	1. Venery.	6. Libidinousness.
Many-worded,		2. Lust.	7. Lecherousness.
Sexual desire.		3. Lechery.	8. Salacity.
		4. Lewdness.	9. Salaciousness.
		5. Lustfulness.	
			10. Venereal desire.

THOMAS ROBERT MALTHUS (1766-1834)

The son of an English country gentleman, Thomas Malthus grew up in Surrey where his education was directed by his father and private tutors. He attended Cambridge University and in 1797 was ordained a minister of the Anglican Church. "Parson" Malthus held a curacy for only a short period; in 1805 he accepted a position as professor of economics at a college founded by the East India Company. The Essay on Population grew out of discussions with his father about certain dreams of a speedy millenium and notions about the perfectibility of mankind held by William Godwin. The now famous Malthusian propositions, posing the practical difficulties that result from excessive population growth, were hastily formulated and published anonymously in 1798. Aware that his arguments were inadequately supported, Malthus travelled abroad from 1799 to 1802, visiting Sweden, Norway, Finland, Russia, Germany, Switzerland and France. In 1803 appeared a second edition, practically a new book, followed by new editions in 1806, 1807, 1817 and 1826. Equally admired and reviled in his day, the amiable parson-turned-economist and his "Malthusian theory of Population" remain, even more today, a subject of violent controversy.

The opening excerpt given below is from the original 1798 edition of the *Essay*; the subsequent chapters are from the fourth (1807) edition.

AN ESSAY ON THE PRINCIPLE OF POPULATION AS IT AFFECTS THE FUTURE IMPROVEMENT OF SOCIETY (1798)

Book I

CHAPTER I

STATEMENT OF RATIOS OF THE INCREASE
OF POPULATION AND FOOD

The great and unlooked for discoveries that have taken place of late years in natural philosophy . . . have all concurred to lead able men into the opinion, that we were touching upon a period big with the most important changes, changes that would in some measure be decisive of the future fate of mankind.

It has been said, that the great question is now at issue, whether man shall henceforth start forwards with accelerated velocity towards illimitable, and hitherto unconceived improvement; or be condemned to a perpetual oscillation between happiness and misery, and after every effort remains still at an immeasurable distance from the wished-for goal. . . .

I have read some of the speculations on the perfectibility of man and of society with great pleasure. I have been warmed and delighted with the enchanting picture which they hold forth. I ardently wish for such happy improvements. But I see great, and, to my understanding, unconquerable difficulties in the way to them. These difficulties it is my present purpose to state; declaring, at the same time, that so far from exulting in them, as a cause of triumphing over the friends of innovation, nothing would give me greater pleasure than to see them completely removed.

The most important argument that I shall adduce is certainly not new. . . . I should certainly, therefore, not think of advancing it again, though I mean to place it in a point of view in some degree different from any that I have hitherto seen, if it had ever been fairly and satisfactorily answered.

The cause of this neglect on the part of the advocates for the perfectibility of mankind is not easily accounted for. I cannot doubt the talents of such men as Godwin and Condorcet. I am unwilling to doubt their candour. To my understanding, and probably to that of most others, the difficulty appears insurmountable. . . .

In entering upon the argument I must premise that I put out of the question, at present, all mere conjectures; that is, all suppositions, the probable realization of which cannot be inferred upon any just philosophical grounds. A writer may tell me that he thinks man will ultimately become an ostrich. I cannot properly contradict him. But before he can expect to bring any reasonable person over to his opinion, he ought to show that the necks of mankind have been gradually elongating; that the lips have grown harder, and more prominent; that the legs and feet are daily altering their shape; and that the hair is beginning to change into stubs of feathers. And till the probability of so wonderful a conversion can be shown, it is surely lost time and lost eloquence to expatiate on the happiness of man in such a state; to describe his powers, both of running and flying; to paint him in a condition where all narrow luxuries would be contemned; where he would be employed, only in collecting the necessaries of life; and where, consequently, each man's share of labour would be light, and his portion of leisure ample.

I think I may fairly make two postulata.

First, That food is necessary to the existence of man.

Secondly, That the passion between the sexes is necessary, and will remain nearly in its present state.

These two laws ever since we have had any knowledge of mankind, appear to have been fixed laws of our nature; and, as we have not hitherto seen any alteration in them, we have no right to conclude that they will ever cease to be what they are now, without an immediate act of power in that Being who first arranged the system of the universe; and for the advantage of his creatures, still executes, according to fixed laws, all its various operations.

I do not know that any writer has supposed that on this earth man will ultimately be able to live without food. But Mr. Godwin has conjectured that the passion between the sexes may in time be extinguished. As, however, he calls this part of his work, a deviation into the land of conjecture, I will not dwell longer upon it at present, than to say, that the best arguments for the perfectibility of man are drawn from a contemplation of the great progress that he has already made from the savage state, and the difficulty of saying where he is to stop. But towards the extinction of the passion between the sexes, no progress whatever has hitherto been made. It appears to exist in as much force at present as it did two thousand, or four thousand years ago. There are individual exceptions now as there always have been. But, as these exceptions do not appear to increase in number, it would surely be a very unphilosophical mode of arguing, to infer merely from the existence of an exception, that the exception would, in time, become the rule, and the rule the exception.

Assuming, then, my postulata as granted, I say, that the power of population is indefinitely greater than the power in the earth to produce subsistence for man.

Population, when unchecked, increases in a geometrical ratio. Subsistence only increases in an arithmetical ratio. A slight acquaintance with numbers will show the immensity of the first power in comparison of the second.

By that law of our nature which makes food necessary to the life of man, the effects of these two unequal powers must be kept equal.

This implies a strong and constantly operating check on population from the difficulty of subsistence. This difficulty must fall some where; and must necessarily be severely felt by a large portion of mankind.

Through the animal and vegetable kingdoms, nature has scattered the seeds of life abroad with the most profuse and liberal hand. She has been comparatively sparing in the room, and the nourishment necessary to rear them. The germs of existence contained in this spot of earth, with ample food, and ample room to expand it, would fill millions of worlds in the course of a few thousand years. Necessity, that imperious, all-pervading law of nature, restrains them within the prescribed bounds. The race of plants, and the race of animals shrink under this great restrictive law. And the race of man cannot, by any efforts of reason, escape from it. Among plants and animals its effects are waste of seed, sickness, and premature death. Among mankind, misery and vice. The former, misery, is an absolutely necessary consequence of it. Vice is a highly probably consequence, and we therefore see it abundantly prevail; but it ought not, perhaps, to be called an absolutely necessary consequence. The ordeal of virtue is to resist all temptation to evil.

This natural inequality of two powers of population, and of production in the earth, and that great law of our nature which must constantly keep their effects equal, form the great difficulty that to me appears insurmountable in the way to perfectibility of society. All other arguments are of slight and subordinate consideration in comparison of this. I see no way by which man can escape from the weight of this law which pervades all animated nature. No fancied equality, no agrarian regulations in their utmost extent, could remove the pressure of it even for a single century. And it appears, therefore, to be decisive against the possible existence of a society, all the members of which should live in ease, happiness, and comparative leisure; and feel no anxiety about providing the means of subsistence for themselves and families.

Consequently, if the premises are just, the argument is conclusive against the perfectibility of the mass of mankind.

I have thus sketched the general outline of the argument; but I will examine it more particularly; and I think it will be found that experience, the true source and foundation of all knowledge, invariably confirms its truth.

CHAPTER II

OF THE GENERAL CHECKS TO POPULATION, AND

THE MODE OF THEIR OPERATION

The ultimate check to population appears then to be a want of food arising necessarily from the different ratios according to which population and food increase. But this ultimate check is never the immediate check, except in cases of actual famine.

The immediate check may be stated to consist in all those customs, and all those diseases which seem to be generated by a scarcity of the means of subsistence; and all those causes, independent of this scarcity, whether of a moral or physical nature, which tend prematurely to weaken and destroy the human frame.

These checks to population, which are constantly operating with more or less force in every society, and keep down the number to the level of the means of subsistence, may be classed under two general heads—the preventive and the positive checks.

The preventive check, as far as it is voluntary, is peculiar to man, and arises from that distinctive superiority in his reasoning faculties which enables him to calculate distant consequences. The checks to the indefinite increase of plants and irrational animals are all either positive, or, if preventive, involuntary. But man cannot look around him and see the distress which frequently presses upon those who have large families; he cannot contemplate his present possessions or earnings, which he now nearly consumes himself and calculate the amount of each share, when with very little addition they must be divided, perhaps, among seven or eight, without feeling a doubt whether, if he follow the bent of his inclinations, he may be able to support the offspring which he will probably bring into the world. In a state of equality, if such can exist, this would be the simple question. In the present state of society other considerations occur. Will he not lower his rank in life, and be obliged to give up in greater measure his former habits? Does any mode of employment present itself by which he may reasonably hope to maintain a family? Will he not at any rate subject himself to greater difficulties, and more severe labour, than in his single state? Will he not be unable to transmit to his children the same advantages of education and improvement that he had himself possessed? Does he even feel secure that, should he have a large family, his utmost exertions can save them from rags and squalid poverty, and their consequent degradation in the community? And may he not be reduced to the grating necessity of forfeiting his independence, and of being obliged to the sparing hand of Charity for support?

These considerations are calculated to prevent, and certainly do prevent, a great number of persons in all civilised nations from pursuing the dictate of nature in an early attachment to one woman.

If this restraint do not produce vice, it is undoubtedly the least evil that can arise from the principle of population. Considered as a restraint on a strong natural inclination, it must be allowed to produce a certain degree of temporary unhappiness; but evidently slight, compared with the evils which result from any of the other checks to population; and merely of the same nature as many other sacrifices of temporary to permanent gratification, which it is the business of a moral agent continually to make.

When this restraint produces vice, the evils which follow are but too conspicuous. A promiscuous intercourse to such a degree as to prevent the birth of children seems to lower, in the most marked manner, the dignity of human nature. It cannot be without its effect on men, and nothing can be more obvious than its tendency to degrade the female character, and to destroy all its most amiable and distinguishing characteristics. Add to which, that among those unfortunate females, with which all great towns abound, more real distress and aggravated misery are, perhaps, to be found than in any other department of human life.

When a general corruption of morals, with regard to the sex, pervades all the classes of society, its effects must necessarily be to poison the springs of domestic happiness, to weaken conjugal and parental affection, and to lessen the united exertions and ardour of parents in the care and education of their children —effects which cannot take place without a decided diminution of the general happiness and virtue of the society; particularly as the necessity of art in the accomplishment and conduct of intrigues, and in the concealment of their consequences, necessarily leads to many other vices.

The positive checks to population are extremely various, and include every cause, whether arising from vice or misery, which in any degree contributes to shorten the natural duration of human life. Under this head, therefore, may be enumerated all unwholesome occupations, severe labour and exposure to the seasons, extreme poverty, bad nursing of children, great towns, excesses of all kinds, the whole train of common diseases and epidemics, wars, plague, and famine.

On examining these obstacles to the increase of population which I have classed under the heads of preventive and positive checks, it will appear that they are all resolvable into moral restraint, vice, and misery.

Of the preventive checks, the restraint from marriage which is not followed by irregular gratifications may properly be termed moral restraint.

Promiscuous intercourse, unnatural passions, violations of the marriage bed, and improper arts to conceal the consequences of irregular connections, are preventive checks that clearly come under the head of vice.

Of the positive checks, those which appear to arise unavoidably from the laws of nature, may be called exclusively misery; and those which we obviously bring upon ourselves, such as wars, excesses, and many others which it would be in our power to avoid, are of a mixed nature. They are brought upon us by vice, and their consequences are misery.

The sum of all these preventive and positive checks, taken together, forms the immediate check to population; and it is evident that, in every country where the whole of the procreative power cannot be called into action, the preventive and the positive checks must vary inversely as each other; that is, in countries either naturally unhealthy, or subject to a great mortality, from whatever cause it may arise, the preventive check will prevail very little. In those countries, on the contrary, which are naturally healthy, and where the preventive check is found to prevail with considerable force, the positive check will prevail very little, or the mortality be very small.

In every country some of these checks are, with more or less force, in constant operation; yet, notwithstanding their general prevalence, there are few states in which there is not a constant effort in the population to increase beyond the means of subsistence. This constant effort as constantly tends to subject the lower classes of society to distress, and to prevent any great permanent melioration of their condition.

These effects, in the present state of society, seem to be produced in the following manner. We will suppose the means of subsistence in any country just equal to the easy support of its inhabitants. The constant effort towards population, which is found to act even in the most vicious societies, increases the number of people before the means of subsistence are increased. The food, therefore, which before supported eleven millions, must now be divided among eleven millions and a half. The poor consequently must live much worse, and many of them be reduced to severe distress. The number of labourers also being above the proportion of work in the market, the price of labour must tend to fall, while the price of provisions would at the same time tend to rise. The labourer therefore must do more work to earn the same as he did before. During this season of distress, the discouragements to marriage and the difficulty of rearing a family are so great, that the progress of population is retarded. In the meantime, the cheapness of labour, the plenty of labourers, and the necessity of an increased industry among them, encourage cultivators to employ more labour upon their land, to turn up fresh soil, and to manure and improve more completely what is already in tillage, till ultimately the means of subsistence may become in the same proportion to the population as at the period from which we set out. The situation of the labourer being then again tolerably comfortable, the restraints to population are in some degree loosened; and, after a short period, the same retrograde and progressive movements, with respect to happiness, are repeated.

This sort of oscillation will not probably be obvious to common view; and it may be difficult even for the most attentive observer to calculate its periods. Yet that in the generality of old states, some such vibration does exist, though in a much less marked, and in a much more irregular manner, than I have described it, no reflecting man who considers the subject deeply can well doubt.

One principal reason why this oscillation has been less remarked, and less decidedly confirmed by experience than might naturally be expected, is, that the histories of mankind which we possess are, in general, histories only of the higher classes. We have not many accounts, that can be depended upon, of the

manners and customs of that part of mankind, where these retrograde and progressive movements chiefly take place. A satisfactory history of this kind, of one people and of one period, would require the constant and minute attention of many observing minds in local and general remarks on the state of the lower classes of society, and the causes that influenced it; and to draw accurate inferences upon this subject, a succession of such historians for some centuries would be necessary. This branch of statistical knowledge has, of late years, been attended to in some countries, and we may promise ourselves a clearer insight into the internal structure of human society from the progress of these inquiries. But the science may be said yet to be in its infancy, and many of the objects, on which it would be desirable to have information, have been either omitted or not stated with sufficient accuracy. Among these, perhaps, may be reckoned the proportion of the number of adults to the number of marriages; the extent to which vicious customs have prevailed in consequence of the restraints upon matrimony; the comparative mortality among the children of the most distressed part of the community and of those who live rather more at their ease; the variations in the real price of labour; the observable differences in the state of the lower classes of society, with respect to ease and happiness, at different times during a certain period; and very accurate registers of births, deaths, and marriages, which are of the utmost importance in this subject.

A faithful history, including such particulars, would tend greatly to elucidate the manner in which the constant check upon population acts; and would probably prove the existence of the retrograde and progressive movements that have been mentioned; though the times of their vibration must necessarily be rendered irregular from the operation of many interrupting causes; such as, the introduction or failure of certain manufactures; a greater or less prevalent spirit of agricultural enterprise; years of plenty or years of scarcity; wars, sickly seasons, poor laws, emigrations, and other causes of a similar nature.

A circumstance which has, perhaps more than any other, contributed to conceal this oscillation from common view is the difference between the nominal and real price of labour. It very rarely happens that the nominal price of labour universally falls; but we well know that it frequently remains the same while the nominal price of provisions has been gradually rising. This, indeed, will generally be the case if the increase of manufactures and commerce be sufficient to employ the new labourers that are thrown into the market, and to prevent the increased supply from lowering the money-price. But an increased number of labourers receiving the same money-wages will necessarily, by their competition, increase the money-price of corn. This is, in fact, a real fall in the price of labour; and, during this period, the condition of the lower classes of the community must be gradually growing worse. But the farmers and capitalists are growing rich from the real cheapness of labour. Their increasing capitals enable them to employ a greater number of men; and, as the population had probably suffered some check from the greater difficulty of supporting a family, the demand for labour, after a certain period, would be great in proportion to the supply, and its price would of course rise, if left to find its natural level; and thus the wages of labour, and consequently the condition of the lower classes of society, might have progressive and retrograde movements, though the price of labour might never nominally fall.

In savage life, where there is no regular price of labour, it is little to be doubted that similar oscillations took place. When population has increased nearly to the utmost limits of the food, all the preventive and the positive checks will naturally operate with increased force. Vicious habits with respect to the sex will be more general, the exposing of children more frequent, and both the probability and fatality of wars and epidemics will be considerably greater; and these causes will probably continue their operation till the population is sunk below the level of the food; and then the return to comparative plenty will again produce an increase, and, after a certain period, its further progress will again be checked by the same causes.

But without attempting to establish these progressive and retrograde movements in different countries, which would evidently require more minute histories than we possess, and which the progress of civilization naturally tends to counteract, the following propositions are intended to be proved:—

1. Population is necessarily limited by the means of subsistence.

2. Population invariably increases where the means of subsistence increase, unless prevented by some very powerful and obvious checks.

3. ~~These checks,~~ and the checks which repress the superior power of population, and keep its effects on a level with the means of subsistence, are all resolvable into moral restraint, vice, and misery.

The first of these propositions scarcely needs illustration, The second and third will sufficiently be established by a review of the immediate checks to population in the past and present state of society.

This review will be the subject of the following chapters.

Book III

CHAPTER V

OF POOR LAWS

To remedy the frequent distresses of the poor, laws to enforce their relief have been instituted; and in the establishment of a general system of this kind England has particularly distinguished herself. But it is to be feared, that, though it may have alleviated a little the intensity of individual misfortune, it has spread the evil over a much larger surface.

It is a subject often started in conversation, and mentioned always as a matter of great surprise, that, notwithstanding the immense sum which is annually collected for the poor in this country, there is still so much distress among them. Some think that the money must be embezzled for private use; others, that the churchwardens and overseers consume the greatest part of it in feasting. All agree, that somehow or other it must be very ill managed. In short, the fact, that even before the late scarcities three millions were collected annually for the poor, and yet that their distresses were not removed, is the subject of continual astonishment. But a man who looks a little below the surface of things would be much more astonished, if the fact were otherwise than it is observed to be; or even if a collection universally of eighteen shillings in the pound, instead of four, were materially to alter it.

Suppose, that by a subscription of the rich the eighteen pence or two shillings, which men earn now, were made up five shillings: it might be imagined, perhaps, that they would then be able to live comfortably, and have a piece of meat every day for their dinner. But this would be a very false conclusion. The transfer of three additional shillings a day to each labourer would not increase the quantity of meat in the country. There is not at present enough for all to have a moderate share. What would then be the consequence? The competition among the buyers in the market of meat would rapidly raise the price from eight pence or nine pence to two or three shillings in the pound, and the commodity would not be divided among many more than it is at present. When an article is scarce, and cannot be distributed to all, he that can show the most valid patent, that is, he that offers the most money, becomes the possessor. If we can suppose the competition among the buyers of meat to continue long enough for a greater number of cattle to be reared annually, this could only be done at the expense of the corn, which would be a very disadvantageous exchange; for it is well known, that the country could not then support the same population; and when subsistence is scarce in proportion to the number of people, it is of little consequence, whether the lowest members of the society possess two shillings or five. They must, at all events, be reduced to live upon the hardest fare, and in the smallest quantity.

It might be said, perhaps, that the increased number of purchasers in every article would give a spur to productive industry, and that the whole produce of the island would be increased. But the spur that these fancied riches would give to population would more than counter-balance it; and the increased produce would have to be divided among a more than proportionably increased number of people.

A collection from the rich of eighteen shillings in the pound, even if distributed in the most judicious manner, would have an effect similar to that resulting from the supposition which I have just made; and no possible sacrifices of the rich, particularly in money, could for any time prevent the recurrence of distress among the lower members of society, whoever they were. Great changes might indeed be made. The rich might become poor, and some of the poor rich: but while the present proportion between population and food continues, a part of the society must necessarily find it difficult to support a family, and this difficulty will naturally fall on the least fortunate members.

Book IV

Chapter III

OF THE ONLY EFFECTUAL MODE OF IMPROVING
THE CONDITION OF THE POOR

He who publishes a moral code, or system of duties, however firmly he may be convinced of the strong obligation on each individual strictly to conform to it, has never the folly to imagine that it will be universally or even generally practised. But this is no valid objection against the publication of the code. If it were, the same objection would always have applied; we should be totally without general rules; and to the vices of mankind arising from temptation would be added a much longer list than we have at present of vices from ignorance.

Judging merely from the light of nature, if we feel convinced of the misery arising from a redundant population on the one hand, and of the evils and unhappiness, particularly to the female sex, arising from promiscuous intercourse, on the other, I do not see how it is possible for any person who acknowledges the principle of utility as the great criterion of moral rules to escape the conclusion that moral restraint, or the abstaining from marriage till we are in a condition to support a family, with a perfectly moral conduct during that period, is the strict line of duty; and when revelation is taken into the question, this duty undoubtedly receives very powerful confirmation. At the same time I believe that few of my readers can be less sanguine than I am in their expectations of any sudden and great change in the general conduct of man on this subject: and the chief reason why in the last chapter I allowed myself to suppose the universal prevalence of this virtue was, that I might endeavour to remove any imputation on the goodness of the Deity, by showing that the evils arising from the principle of population were exactly of the same nature as the generality of other evils which excite fewer complaints: that they were increased by human ignorance and indolence, and diminished by human knowledge and virtue; and on the supposition that each individual strictly fulfilled his duty would be almost totally removed; and this without any general diminution of those sources of pleasure, arising from the regulated indulgence of the passions, which have been justly considered as the principal ingredients of human happiness.

If it will answer any purpose of illustration, I see no harm in drawing the picture of a society in which each individual is supposed strictly to fulfil his duties; nor does a writer appear to be justly liable to the imputation of being visionary unless he make such universal or general obedience necessary to the practical utility of his system, and to that degree of moderate and partial improvement, which is all that can rationally be expected from the most complete knowledge of our duties.

But in this respect there is an essential difference between that improved state of society, which I have supposed in the last chapter, and most of the other speculations on this subject. The improvement there supposed, if we ever should make approaches towards it, is to be effected in the way in which we have been in the habit of seeing all the greatest improvements effected, by a direct application to the interest and happiness of each individual. It is not required of us to act from motives to which we are unaccustomed; to pursue a general good which we may not distinctly comprehend, or the effect of which may be weakened by distance and diffusion. The happiness of the whole is to be the result of the happiness of individuals, and to begin first with them. No co-operation is required. Every step tells. He who performs his duty faithfully will reap the full fruits of it, whatever may be the number of others who fail. This duty is intelligible to the humblest capacity. It is merely that he is not to bring beings into the world for whom he cannot find the means of support. When once this subject is cleared from the obscurity thrown over it by parochial laws and private benevolence, every man must feel the strongest conviction of such an obligation. If he cannot support his children they must starve; and if he marry in the face of a fair probability that he shall not be able to support his children, he is guilty of all the evils which he thus brings upon himself, his wife, and his offspring. It is clearly his interest, and will tend greatly to promote his happiness, to defer marrying till by industry and economy he is in a capacity to support the children that he may reasonably expect from his marriage; and as he cannot in the meantime gratify his passions without violating an express command of God, and running a great risk of injuring himself, or some of his fellow-creatures, considerations of his own interest and happiness will dictate to him the strong obligation to a moral conduct while he remains unmarried.

However powerful may be the impulses of passion, they are generally in some degree modified by reason. And it does not seem entirely visionary to suppose that, if the true and permanent cause of poverty were clearly explained and forcibly brought home to each man's bosom, it would have some, and perhaps not an inconsiderable influence on his conduct; at least the experiment has never yet been fairly tried. Almost everything that has been hitherto done for the poor has tended, as if with solicitous care, to throw a veil of obscurity over this subject, and to hide from them the true cause of their poverty. When the wages of labour are hardly sufficient to maintain two children, a man marries and has five or six; he of course finds himself miserably distressed. He accuses the insufficiency of the price of labour to maintain a family. He accuses his parish for their tardy and sparing fulfilment of their obligation to assist him. He accuses the avarice of the rich, who suffer him to want what they can so well spare. He accuses the partial and unjust institutions of society, which have awarded him an inadequate share of the produce of the earth. He accuses perhaps the dispensations of Providence, which have assigned to him a place in society so beset with unavoidable distress and dependence. In searching for objects of accusation, he never adverts to the quarter from which his misfortunes originate. The last person that he would think of accusing is himself, on whom in fact the principal blame lies, except so far as he has been deceived by the higher classes of society. He may perhaps wish that he had not married, because he now feels the inconveniences of it; but it never enters into his head that he can have done anything wrong. He has always been told that to raise up subjects for his king and country is a very meritorious act. He has done this, and yet is suffering for it; and it cannot but strike him as most extremely unjust and cruel in his king and country to allow him thus to suffer, in return for giving them what they are continually declaring that they particularly want.

Till these erroneous ideas have been corrected, and the language of nature and reason has been generally heard on the subject of population, instead of the language of error and prejudice, it cannot be said that any fair experiment has been made with the understandings of the common people; and we cannot justly accuse them of improvidence and want of industry till they act as they do now after it has been brought home to their comprehensions that they are themselves the cause of their own poverty; that the means of redress are in their own hands, and in the hands of no other persons whatever; that the society in which they live and the government which presides over it are without any *direct* power in this respect; and that however ardently they may desire to relieve them, and whatever attempts they may make to do so, they are really and truly unable to execute what they benevolently wish, but unjustly promise; that, when the wages of labour will not maintain a family, it is an incontrovertible sign that their king and country do not want more subjects, or at least that they cannot support them; that if they marry in this case, so far from fulfilling a duty to society, they are throwing a useless burden on it, at the same time that they are plunging themselves into distress; and that they are acting directly contrary to the will of God, and bring down upon themselves various diseases, which might all, or the greater part, have been avoided if they had attended to the repeated admonitions which he gives by the general laws of nature to every being capable of reason.

Paley, in his Moral Philosophy, observes that in countries "in which subsistence is become scarce, it behoves the state to watch over the public morals with increased solicitude; for nothing but the instinct of nature, under the restraint of chastity, will induce men to undertake the labour, or consent to the sacrifice of personal liberty and indulgence, which the support of a family in such circumstances requires." That it is always the duty of a state to use every exertion likely to be effectual in discouraging vice and promoting virtue, and that no temporary circumstances ought to cause any relaxation in these exertions, is certainly true. The means therefore proposed are always good; but the particular end in view in this case appears to be absolutely criminal. We wish to force people into marriage when from the acknowledged scarcity of subsistence they will have little chance of being able to support their children. We might as well force people into the water who are unable to swim. In both cases we rashly tempt Providence. Nor have we more reason to believe that a miracle will be worked to save us from the misery and mortality resulting from our conduct in the one case than in the other.

The object of those who really wish to better the condition of the lower classes of society must be to raise the relative proportion between the price of labour and the price of provisions, so as to enable the labourer to command a larger share of the necessaries and comforts of life. We have hitherto principally attempted to attain this end by encouraging the married poor, and consequently increasing the number of labourers, and overstocking the market with a commodity which we still say that we wish to be dear. It would seem to have required no great spirit of divination to foretell the certain failure of such a plan of proceeding. There is nothing however like experience. It has been tried in many different countries, and for many hundred years, and the success has always been answerable to the nature of the scheme. It is really time now to try something else.

When it was found that oxygen, or pure vital air, would not cure consumptions as was expected, but rather aggravated their symptoms, trial was made of an air of the most opposite kind. I wish we had acted with the same philosophical spirit in our attempts to cure the disease of poverty; and having found that the pouring in of fresh supplies of labour only tended to aggravate the symptoms, had tried what would be the effect of withholding a little of these supplies.

In all old and fully-peopled states it is from this method, and this alone, that we can rationally expect any essential and permanent amelioration in the condition of the labouring classes of the people.

In an endeavour to raise the proportion of the quantity of provisions to the number of consumers in any country, our attention would naturally be first directed to the increasing of the absolute quantity of provisions; but finding that, as fast as we did this, the number of consumers more than kept pace with it, and that with all our exertions we were still as far as ever behind, we should be convinced that our efforts directed only in this way would never succeed. It would appear to be setting the tortoise to catch the hare. Finding, therefore, that from the laws of nature we could not proportion the food to the population, our next attempt should naturally be to proportion the population to the food. If we can persuade the hare to go to sleep, the tortoise may have some chance of overtaking her.

We are not, however, to relax our efforts in increasing the

quantity of provisions, but to combine another effort with it; that of keeping the population, when once it has been overtaken, at such a distance behind as to effect the relative proportion which we desire; and thus unite the two grand *desiderata,* a great actual population and a state of society in which abject poverty and dependence are comparatively but little known; two objects which are far from being incompatible.

If we be really serious in what appears to be object of such general research, the mode of essentially and permanently bettering the condition of the poor, we must explain to them the true nature of their situation, and show them that the withholding of the supplies of labour is the only possible way of really raising its price, and that they themselves, being the possessors of this commodity, have alone the power to do this.

I cannot but consider this mode of diminishing poverty as so perfectly clear in theory, and so invariably confirmed by the analogy of every other commodity which is brought to market, that nothing but its being shown to be calculated to produce greater evils than it proposes to remedy can justify us in not making the attempt to put it into execution.

CHAPTER V

OF THE CONSEQUENCES OF PURSUING THE OPPOSITE MODE

It is an evident truth that, whatever may be the rate of increase in the means of subsistence, the increase of population must be limited by it, at least after the food has once been divided into the smallest shares that will support life. All the children born beyond what would be required to keep up the population to this level must necessarily perish, unless room be made for them by the deaths of grown persons. It has appeared indeed clearly in the course of this work that in all old states the marriages and births depend principally upon the deaths, and that there is no encouragement to early unions so powerful as a great mortality. To act consistently, therefore, we should facilitate, instead of foolishly and vainly endeavouring to impede, the operations of nature in producing this mortality; and if we dread the too frequent visitation of the horrid form of famine, we should sedulously encourage the other forms of destruction which we compel nature to use. Instead of recommending cleanliness to the poor, we should encourage contrary habits. In our towns we should make the streets narrower, crowd more people into the houses, and court the return of the plague. In the country, we should build our villages near stagnant pools, and particularly encourage settlements in all marshy and unwholesome situations. But above all, we should reprobate specific remedies for ravaging diseases; and those benevolent, but much mistaken men, who have thought they were doing a service to mankind by projecting schemes for the total extirpation of particular disorders. If by these and similar means the annual mortality were increased from 1 in 36 or 40, to 1 in 18 or 20, we might probably every one of us marry at the age of puberty, and yet few be absolutely starved.

If, however, we all marry at this age, and yet still continue our exertions to impede the operations of nature, we may rest assured that all our efforts will be vain. Nature will not, nor cannot, be defeated in her purposes. The necessary mortality must come in some form or other; and the extirpation of one disease will only be the signal for the birth of another perhaps more fatal. We cannot lower the waters of misery by pressing them down in different places, which must necessarily make them rise somewhere else; the only way in which we can hope to effect our purpose is by drawing them off. To this course nature is constantly directing our attention by the chastisements which await a contrary conduct. These chastisements are more or less severe in proportion to the degree in which her admonitions produce their intended effect. In this country at present these admonitions are by no means entirely neglected. The preventive check to population prevails to a considerable degree, and her chastisements are in consequence moderate; but if we were all to marry at the age of puberty they would be severe indeed. Political evils would probably be added to physical. A people goaded by constant distress, and visited by frequent returns of famine, could not be kept down but by a cruel despotism. We should approach to the state of the people in Egypt or Abyssinia; and I would ask whether in that case it is probable that we should be more virtuous? . . .

If, on contemplating the increase of vice which might contingently follow an attempt to inculcate the duty of moral restraint, and the increase of misery that must necessarily follow the attempts to encourage marriage and population, we come to the conclusion not to interfere in any respect, but to leave every man to his own free choice, and responsible only to God for the evil which he does in either way; this is all I contend for; I would on no account do more; but I contend that at present we are very far from doing this.

Among the lower classes of society, where the point is of the greatest importance, the poor-laws afford a direct, constant, and systematical encouragement to marriage, by removing from each individual that heavy responsibility, which he would incur by the laws of nature, for bringing beings into the world which he could not support. Our private benevolence has the same direction as the poor-laws, and almost invariably tends to encourage marriage, and to equalise as much as possible the circumstances of married and single men.

Among the higher classes of people, the superior distinctions which married women receive, and the marked inattentions to which single women of advanced age are exposed, enable many men, who are agreeable neither in mind nor person, and are besides in the wane of life, to choose a partner among the young and fair, instead of being confined, as nature seems to dictate, to persons of nearly their own age and accomplishments. It is scarcely to be doubted that the fear of being an old maid, and of that silly and unjust ridicule, which folly sometimes attaches to this name, drives many women into the marriage union with men whom they dislike, or at best to whom they are perfectly indifferent. Such marriages must to every delicate mind appear little better than legal prostitutions; and they often burden the earth with unnecessary children, without compensating for it by an accession of happiness and virtue to the parties themselves.

Throughout all the ranks of society the prevailing opinions respecting the duty and obligation of marriage cannot but have a very powerful influence. The man who thinks that, in going out of the world without leaving representatives behind him, he shall have failed in an important duty to society, will be disposed to force rather than to repress his inclinations on this subject; and when his reason represents to him the difficulties attending a family, he will endeavour not to attend to these suggestions, will still determine to venture, and will hope that, in the discharge of what he conceives to be his duty, he shall not be deserted by Providence.

In a civilised country, such as England, where a taste for the decencies and comforts of life prevails among a very large class of people, it is not possible that the encouragements to marriage from positive institutions and prevailing opinions should entirely obscure the light of nature and reason on this subject; but still they contribute to make it comparatively weak and indistinct. And till this obscurity is removed, and the poor are undeceived with respect to the principal cause of their poverty, and taught to know that their happiness or misery must depend chiefly upon themselves, it cannot be said that, with regard to the great question of marriage, we leave every man to his own free and fair choice.

DAVID RICARDO (1772-1823)

Unlike Malthus, who knew nothing of the business world, David Ricardo was a phenomenally successful manipulator of the money market. The son of a Dutch banker who had emigrated to London, the young Ricardo went to work for his father at the age of fourteen. Marriage to a gentile led to a break with his orthodox Jewish family and an independent business career. Within a few years he had amassed a fortune on the Exchange; then he turned to the study of economics, breaking into print in 1809 with an article on the bullion controversy. His major work, *On the Principles of Political Economy and Taxation,* appeared in 1817 and assured his place as the leading economist of his day. Elected to Parliament in 1819, he retained his seat until his death in 1823. Although a poor speaker and a difficult writer to comprehend, his reputation as a financial wizard and his recognized intellectual superiority always won him a respectful audience.

The selections given below are from the third edition of the *Principles* published in 1821.

PRINCIPLES OF POLITICAL ECONOMY AND TAXATION (1817)

CHAPTER I

ON VALUE

The value of a commodity, or the quantity of any other commodity for which it will exchange, depends on the relative quantity of labour which is necessary for its production, and not on the greater or less compensation which is paid for that labour.

It has been observed by Adam Smith, that "the word Value has two different meanings, and sometimes expresses the utility of some particular object, and sometimes the power of purchasing other goods which the possession of that object conveys. The one may be called *value in use;* the other *value in exchange.* The things," he continues, "which have the greatest value in use, have frequently little or no value in exchange; and, on the contrary, those which have the greatest value in exchange, have little or no value in use." Water and air are abundantly useful; they are indeed indispensable to existence, yet, under ordinary circumstances, nothing can be obtained in exchange for them. Gold, on the contrary, though of little use compared with air or water, will exchange for a great quantity of other goods.

Utility then is not the measure of exchangeable value, although it is absolutely essential to it. If a commodity were in no way useful,—in other words, if it could in no way contribute to our gratification,—it would be destitute of exchangeable value, however scarce it might be, or whatever quantity of labour might be necessary to procure it.

Possessing utility, commodities derive their exchangeable value from two sources: from their scarcity, and from the quantity of labour required to obtain them.

There are some commodities, the value of which is determined by their scarcity alone. No labour can increase the quantity of such goods, and therefore their value cannot be lowered by an increased supply. Some rare statues and pictures, scarce books and coins, wines of a peculiar quality, which can be made only from grapes grown on a particular soil, of which there is a very limited quantity, are all of this description. Their value is wholly independent of the quantity of labour originally necessary to produce them, and varies with the varying wealth and inclinations of those who are desirous to possess them.

These commodities, however, form a very small part of the mass of commodities daily exchanged in the market. By far the greatest part of those goods which are the objects of desire, are procured by labour; and they may be multiplied, not in one country alone, but in many, almost without any assignable limit, if we are disposed to bestow the labour necessary to obtain them.

In speaking then of commodities, of their exchangeable value, and of the laws which regulate their relative prices, we mean always such commodities only as can be increased in quantity by the exertion of human industry, and on the production of which competition operates without restraint. . . .

If the quantity of labour realized in commodities, regulate their exchangeable value, every increase of the quantity of labour must augment the value of that commodity on which it is exercised, as every diminution must lower it. . . .

CHAPTER II

ON RENT

It remains however to be considered, whether the appropriation of land, and the consequent creation of rent, will occasion any variation in the relative value of commodities, independently of the quantity of labour necessary to production. In order to understand this part of the subject, we must enquire into the nature of rent, and the laws by which its rise or fall is regulated.

Rent is that portion of the produce of the earth, which is paid to the landlord for the use of the original and indestructible powers of the soil. . . .

On the first settling of a country, in which there is an abundance of rich and fertile land, a very small proportion of which is required to be cultivated for the support of the actual population, or indeed can be cultivated with the capital which the population can command, there will be no rent; for no one would pay for the use of land, when there was an abundant quantity not yet appropriated, and, therefore, at the disposal of whosoever might choose to cultivate it.

On the common principles of supply and demand, no rent could be paid for such land, for the reason stated why nothing is given for the use of air and water, or for any other of the gifts of nature which exist in boundless quantity. . . . If all land had the same properties, if it were unlimited in quantity, and uniform in quality, no charge could be made for its use, unless where it possessed peculiar advantages of situation. It is only, then, because land is not unlimited in quantity and uniform in quality, and because in the progress of population, land of an inferior quality, or less advantageously situated, is called into cultivation, that rent is ever paid for the use of it. When in the progress of society, land of the second degree of fertility is taken into cultivation, rent immediately commences on that of the first quality, and the amount of that rent will depend on the difference in the quality of these two portions of land.

When land of the third quality is taken into cultivation, rent immediately commences on the second, and it is regulated as before, by the difference in their productive powers. At the same time, the rent of the first quality will rise, for that must always be above the rent of the second, by the difference between the produce which they yield with a given quantity of capital and labour. With every step in the progress of population, which shall oblige a country to have recourse to land of a worse quality, to enable it to raise its supply of food, rent, on all the more fertile land, will rise.

Thus suppose land—No. 1, 2, 3—to yield, with an equal

employment of capital and labour, a net produce of 100, 90, and 80 quarters of corn. In a new country, where there is an abundance of fertile land compared with the population, and where therefore it is only necessary to cultivate No. 1, the whole net produce will belong to the cultivator, and will be the profits of the stock which he advances. As soon as population had so far increased as to make it necessary to cultivate No. 2, from which ninety quarters only can be obtained after supporting the labourers, rent would commence on No. 1; for either there must be two rates of profit on agricultural capital, or ten quarters, or the value of ten quarters must be withdrawn from the produce of No. 1, for some other purpose. Whether the proprietor of the land or any other person, cultivated No. 1, these ten quarters would equally constitute rent; for the cultivator of No. 2 would get the same result with his capital, whether he cultivated No. 1, paying ten quarters for rent, or continued to cultivate No. 2, paying no rent. In the same manner it might be shown that when No. 3 is brought into cultivation, the rent of No. 2 must be ten quarters, or the value of ten quarters, whilst the rent of No. 1 would rise to twenty quarters; for the cultivator of No. 3 would have the same profits whether he paid twenty quarters for the rent of No. 1, ten quarters for the rent of No. 2, or cultivated No. 3 free of all rent. . . .

The most fertile, and most favourably situated, land will be first cultivated, and the exchangeable value of its produce will be adjusted in the same manner as the exchangeable value of all other commodities, by the total quantity of labour necessary in various forms from first to last, to produce it, and bring it to market. When land of an inferior quality is taken into cultivation, the exchangeable value of raw produce will rise, because more labour is required to produce it.

The exchangeable value of all commodities, whether they be manufactured, or the produce of the mines, or the produce of the land, is always regulated, not by the less quantity of labour that will suffice for their production under circumstances highly favourable, and exclusively enjoyed by those who have peculiar facilities of production; but by the greater quantity of labour necessarily bestowed on their production by those who have no such facilities; by those who continue to produce them under the most unfavourable circumstances; meaning—by the most unfavourable circumstances, the most unfavourable under which the quantity of produce required, renders it necessary to carry on the production. . . .

It is true, that on the best land, the same produce would still be obtained with the same labour as before, but its value would be enhanced in consequence of the diminished returns obtained by those who employed fresh labour and stock on the less fertile land. Notwithstanding, then, that the advantages of fertile over inferior lands are in no case lost, but only transferred from the cultivator, or consumer, to the landlord, yet, since more labour is required on the inferior lands, and since it is from such land that we are enabled to furnish ourselves with the additional supply of raw produce, the comparative value of that produce will continue permanently above its former level, and make it exchange for more hats, cloth, shoes, etc., etc., in the production of which no such additional quantity of labour is required.

The reason then, why raw produce rises in comparative value, is because more labour is employed in the production of the last portion obtained, and not because a rent is paid to the landlord. The value of corn is regulated by the quantity of labour bestowed on its production on that quality of land, or with that portion of capital, which pays no rent. Corn is not high because a rent is paid, but a rent is paid because corn is high; and it has been justly observed, that no reduction would take place in the price of corn, although landlords should forego the whole of their rent. Such a measure would only enable some farmers to live like gentlemen, but would not diminish the quantity of labour necessary to raise raw produce on the least productive land in cultivation.

Nothing is more common than to hear of the advantages which the land possesses over every other source of useful produce, on account of the surplus which it yields in the form of rent. Yet when land is most abundant, when most productive, and most fertile, it yields no rent; and it is only when its powers decay, and less is yielded in return for labour, that a share of the original produce of the more fertile portions is set apart for rent. . . .

The rise of rent is always the effect of the increasing wealth of the country, and of the difficulty of providing food for its augmented population. It is a symptom, but it is never a cause of wealth; for wealth often increases most rapidly while rent is either stationary, or even falling. Rent increases most rapidly, as the disposible land decreases in its productive powers. Wealth increases most rapidly in those countries where the disposable land is most fertile, where importation is least restricted, and where, through agricultural improvements, productions can be multiplied without any increase in the proportional quantity of labour, and where consequently the progress of rent is slow. . . .

In speaking of the rent of the landlord, we have rather considered it as the proportion of the produce, obtained with a given capital on any given farm, without any reference to its exchangeable value; but since the same cause, the difficulty of production, raises the exchangeable value of raw produce, and raises also the proportion of raw produce paid to the landlord for rent, it is obvious that the landlord is doubly benefited by the difficulty of production. First, he obtains a greater share, and, secondly, the commodity in which he is paid is of greater value.

Chapter V
on wages

Labour, like all other things which are purchased and sold, and which may be increased or diminished in quantity, has its natural and its market price. The natural price of labour is that price which is necessary to enable the labourers, one with another, to subsist and to perpetuate their race, without either increase or diminution.

The power of the labourer to support himself, and the family which may be necessary to keep up the number of labourers, does not depend on the quantity of money which he may receive for wages, but on the quantity of food, necessaries, and conveniences become essential to him from habit which that money will purchase. The natural price of labour, therefore, depends on the price of the food, necessaries, and conveniences required for the support of the labourer and his family. With a rise in the price of food and necessaries, the natural price of labour will rise; with the fall in their price, the natural price of labour will fall.

With the progress of society the natural price of labour has always a tendency to rise, because one of the principal commodities by which its natural price is regulated has a tendency to become dearer from the greater difficulty of producing it. As, however, the improvements in agriculture, the discovery of new markets, whence provisions may be imported, may for a time counteract the tendency to a rise in the price of necessaries, and may even occasion their natural price to fall, so will the same causes produce the correspondent effects on the natural price of labour.

The natural price of all commodities, excepting raw produce and labour, has a tendency to fall in the progress of wealth and population; for though, on one hand, they are enhanced in real value, from the rise in the natural price of the raw material of which they are made, this is more than counterbalanced by the improvements in machinery, by the better division and distribution of labour, and by the increasing skill, both in science and art, of the producers.

The market price of labour is the price which is really paid for it, from the natural operation of the proportion of the supply to the demand; labour is dear when it is scarce and cheap when it is plentiful. However much the market price of labour may deviate from its natural price, it has, like commodities, a tendency to conform to it.

It is when the market price of labour exceeds its natural price that the condition of the labourer is flourishing and happy, that he has it in his power to command a greater proportion of the necessaries and enjoyments of life, and therefore to rear a healthy and numerous family. When, however, by the encouragement which high wages give to the increase of population, the number of labourers is increased, wages again fall to their natural price, and indeed from a reaction sometimes fall below it.

When the market price of labour is below its natural price, the condition of the labourers is most wretched: then poverty deprives them of those comforts which custom renders absolute necessaries. It is only after their privations have reduced their number, or the demand for labour has increased, that the market price of labour will rise to its natural price, and that the labourer will have the moderate comforts which the natural rate of wages will afford. . . .

It is not to be understood that the natural price of labour, estimated even in food and necessaries, is absolutely fixed and constant. It varies at different times in the same country, and very materially differs in different countries. It essentially depends on the habits and customs of the people. An English labourer would consider his wages under their natural rate, and too scanty to support a family, if they enabled him to purchase no other food than potatoes, and to live in no better habitation than a mud cabin; yet these moderate demands of nature are often deemed sufficient in countries where "man's life is cheap" and his wants easily satisfied. Many of the conveniences now enjoyed in an English cottage would have been thought luxuries at an earlier period of our history.

From manufactured commodities always falling and raw produce always rising, with the progress of society, such a dis-proportion in their relative value is at length created, that in rich countries a labourer, by the sacrifice of a very small quantity only of his food, is able to provide liberally for all his other wants.

Independently of the variations in the value of money, which necessarily affect money wages, but which we have here sup-posed to have no operation, as we have considered money to be uniformly of the same value, it appears then that wages are sub-ject to a rise or fall from two causes:—

First, the supply and demand of labourers.

Secondly, the price of the commodities on which the wages of labour are expended.

In different stages of society, the accumulation of capital, or of the means of employing labour, is more or less rapid, and must in all cases depend on the productive powers of labour. The productive powers of labour are generally greatest when there is an abundance of fertile land: at such periods accumulation is often so rapid that labourers cannot be supplied with the same rapidity as capital.

It has been calculated that under favourable circumstances population may be doubled in twenty-five years; but under the same favourable circumstances the whole capital of a country might possibly be doubled in a shorter period. In that case, wages during the whole period would have a tendency to rise, because the demand for labour would increase still faster than the supply.

In new settlements, where the arts and knowledge of coun-tries far advanced in refinement are introduced, it is probable that capital has a tendency to increase faster than mankind; and if the deficiency of labourers were not supplied by more populous countries, this tendency would very much raise the price of labour. In proportion as these countries become populous, and land of a worse quality is taken into cultivation, the tendency to an increase of capital diminishes; for the surplus produce remaining, after satisfying the wants of the existing population, must necessarily be in proportion to the facility of production, viz. to the smaller number of persons employed in production. Although, then, it is probable that, under the most favourable circumstances, the power of production is still greater than that of population, it will not long continue so; for the land being limited in quantity, and differing in quality, with every increased portion of capital employed on it there will be a decreased rate of production, whilst the power of population continues always the same.

With a population pressing against the means of subsistence, the only remedies are either a reduction of people or a more rapid accumulation of capital. In rich countries, where all the fertile land is already cultivated, the latter remedy is neither very practicable nor very desirable, because its effect would be, if pushed very far, to render all classes equally poor. But in poor countries, where there are abundant means of production in store, from fertile land not yet brought into cultivation, it is the only safe and efficacious means of removing the evil, particularly as its effect would be to elevate all classes of the people.

The friends of humanity cannot but wish that in all countries the labouring classes should have a taste for comforts and enjoyments, and that they should be stimulated by all legal means in their exertions to procure them. There cannot be a better security against a super-abundant population. In those countries where the labouring classes have the fewest wants, and are contented with the cheapest food, the people are exposed to the greatest vicissitudes and miseries. They have no place of refuge from calamity; they cannot seek safety in a lower station; they are already so low that they can fall no lower. On any deficiency of the chief article of their subsistence there are few substitutes of which they can avail themselves and dearth to them is attended with almost all the evils of famine.

In the natural advance of society, the wages of labour will

have a tendency to fall, as far as they are regulated by supply and demand; for the supply of labourers will continue to increase at the same rate, whilst the demand for them will increase at a slower rate. . . . I say that, under these circumstances, wages would fall if they were regulated only by the supply and demand of labourers; but we must not forget that wages are also regulated by the prices of the commodities on which they are expended.

As population increases, these necessaries will be constantly rising in price, because more labour will be necessary to produce them. If, then, the money wages of labour should fall, whilst every commodity on which the wages of labour were expended rose, the labourer would be doubly affected, and would be soon totally deprived of subsistence. Instead, therefore, of the money wages of labour falling, they would rise; but they would not rise sufficiently to enable the labourer to purchase as many comforts and necessaries as he did before the rise in the price of those commodities. . . .

Notwithstanding, then, that the labourer would be really worse paid, yet this increase in his wages would necessarily diminish the profits of the manufacturer; for his goods would sell at no higher price, and yet the expense of producing them would be increased. This, however, will be considered in our examination into the principles which regulate profits.

It appears, then, that the same cause which raises rent, namely, the increasing difficulty of providing an additional quantity of food with the same proportional quantity of labour, will also raise wages; and therefore, if money be of an unvarying value, both rent and wages will have a tendency to rise with the progress of wealth and population.

But there is this essential difference between the rise of rent and the rise of wages. The rise in the money value of rent is accompanied by an increased share of the produce; not only is the landlord's money rent greater, but his corn rent also; he will have more corn, and each defined measure of that corn will exchange for a greater quantity of all other goods which have not been raised in value. The fate of the labourer will be less happy; he will receive more money wages, it is true, but his corn wages will be reduced; and not only his command of corn, but his general condition will be deteriorated, by his finding it more difficult to maintain the market rate of wages above their natural rate. While the price of corn rises 10 per cent., wages will always rise less than 10 per cent., but rent will always rise more; the condition of the labourer will generally decline, and that of the landlord will always be improved. . . .

These, then, are the laws by which wages are regulated, and by which the happiness of far the greatest part of every community is governed. Like all other contracts, wages should be left to the fair and free competition of the market, and should never be controlled by the interference of the legislature.

The clear and direct tendency of the poor laws is in direct opposition to these obvious principles: it is not, as the legislature benevolently intended, to amend the condition of the poor, but to deteriorate the condition of both poor and rich; instead of making the poor rich, they are calculatd to make the rich poor; and whilst the present laws are in force, it is quite in the natural order of things that the fund for the maintenance of the poor should progressively increase till it has absorbed all the net revenue of the country, or at least so much of it as the state shall leave to us, after satisfying its own never-failing demands for the public expenditure.

This pernicious tendency of these laws is no longer a mystery, since it has been fully developed by the able hand of Mr. Malthus; and every friend to the poor must ardently wish for their abolition. Unfortunately, however, they have been so long established, and the habits of the poor have been so formed upon their operation, that to eradicate them with safety from our political system requires the most cautious and skilful management. It is agreed by all who are most friendly to a repeal of these laws that, if it be desirable to prevent the most overwhelming distress to those for whose benefit they were erroneously enacted, their abolition should be effected by the most gradual steps.

It is truth which admits not a doubt that the comforts and well-being of the poor cannot be permanently secured without some regard on their part, or some effort on the part of the legislature, to regulate the increase of their numbers, and to render less frequent among them early and improvident marriages. The operation of the system of poor laws has been directly contrary to this. They have rendered restraint superfluous, and have invited imprudence, by offering it a portion of the wages of prudence and industry.

The nature of the evil points out the remedy. By gradually contracting the sphere of the poor laws; by impressing on the poor the value of independence, by teaching them that they must look not to systematic or casual charity, but to their own exertions for support, that prudence and forethought are neither unnecessary not unprofitable virtues, we shall by degrees approach a sounder and more healthful state.

No scheme for the amendment of the poor laws merits the least attention which has not their abolition for its ultimate object; and he is the best friend of the poor, and to the cause of humanity, who can point out how this end can be attained with the most security, and at the same time with the least violence. . . . If by law every human being wanting support could be sure to obtain it, and obtain it in such a degree as to make life tolerably comfortable, theory would lead us to expect that all other taxes together would be light compared with the single one of poor rates. The principle of gravitation is not more certain than the tendency of such laws to change wealth and power into misery and weakness; to call away the exertions of labour from every object, except that of providing mere subsistence; to confound all intellectual distinction; to busy the mind continually in supplying the body's wants; until at last all classes should be infected with the plague of universal poverty. . . .

CHILD LABOR IN FACTORIES AND MINES

The seamy side of the industrial revolution was graphically presented to members of Parliament and the reading public of Great Britain through three comprehensive, and justly famous, official reports. The first, by the Sadler Committee, followed hearings held in 1832 to investigate conditions of child labor in the textile mills; the second, by Lord Ashley's Mines Commission in 1842, dealt with working conditions in the mines with emphasis on child labor in the coal pits; the third, also in 1842, under Edwin Chadwick, concerned itself with "the Sanitary Conditions of the Labouring Population." The reader will note the committees' tendency to ask leading questions of the witnesses, and the reports have been criticized on this ground. Slanted or not, the committee findings shocked the British public into demanding remedial legislation. An Act passed in 1833 limited hours for women and children in textile factories, and one of 1842 prohibited employment in mines of all women and of boys under thirteen.

The testimony given below, from the first two reports, is drawn from *Parliamentary Papers*, 1831-32, vol. XV and 1842, vols. XV-XVII.

TESTIMONY PRESENTED TO THE SADLER COMMITTEE (1832)

Joshua Drake, called in; and examined

What is your business? — A woollen weaver.

Where do you reside? — At Leeds.

You say that you had a child that went to the flax-mill and she was between 14 and 15; do they take them in as early into the flax-mills as into the woollen mills? — Yes; but it was not my idea to send her to a flax-mill; it was her own wish; owing to some comrades that she had working at Mr. Benyon's.

Was she a healthy girl? — She was very healthy when she went there. Was it the dust that injured her health? — Whether it was the dust, or being sometimes over-worked till she sweated, and then chilling again, I cannot say.

What sort of room was it she worked in? — I was never in it, but when she came out she was covered with dust and flyings of tow.

Did she ever tell you whether the nature of her work was such as to make her very hot? — No; but she said that sometimes they were made to sweat a good deal, and that they starved, and then this dust choked her; but it was not above three or four days before it was very visible that this dust had an effect upon her, and she fell sick.

Did she suffer more from it than her companions? — I do not know whether she did or not, but I think that of the four girls who were her comrades, three of them are dead.

You say that you were in the habit of giving her a vomit once a week? — Yes; it was by the advice of the people that had children working at the flax-mills.

Was it by the advice of any medical man? — No; but it is a practice that is continued now. I have a brother-in-law now that has a child working at it, and they give her a sort of vomit of salts once a week, to relieve her stomach.

You say she was beaten several times, did she ever say what she was beaten for? — For some neglect, and the tow not being properly thick; I think she said, the overlooker said she was spreading it too thick, and he knocked her down, and beat her, and I took her away; they sent word that she should be shifted to another overlooker if she would go.

Is it not necessary in those mills, as in other places where children are employed, to have some means of keeping them in order? — They must be kept in order so as to mind their work; but I always found that the best-tempered slubbers generally get the best warps done.

When the child is corrected in this way, is it upon the complaint of the slubber? — The slubber has it in his own management either to correct or to screen; the overlooker seldom meddles with the children, except where the slubber complains; and then if he be a bad-tempered overlooker, he takes them and beats them himself. But as far as ever I knew, the best-tempered slubbers have always the least complaint of their work.

What means would you suggest of putting a stop to this cruel treatment? — If the law could do anything for it, I would have them punished by law as for assault; where the assault leaves a visible mark.

Are you aware whether there is any provision of that sort in the Bill? — No, I do not know anything about it; but I know this, that there was a boy taken and tied upon another man's back, and they flogged him round the place; and he was brought down to Leeds Court-house, and the mayor, after looking at the child, ordered the offender to go out and make it up with the parent of the boy, or otherwise he would be punished.

So that, in short, if they ill-treated a child now, the magistrates would punish them? — They will let him compromise for a few shillings.

But does not that rest with the option of the parent? — The child's father was obliged to it; but I think he got seven or eight shillings.

Do you not think that those children were generally more cruelly treated at the termination of the day, when they have over-laboured themselves, and are actually fatigued? — Yes.

Is it not found by universal experience, that the most cruel punishments take place when undue hours of labour are imposed upon the children, and, when, therefore, they are no longer able to perform the work? — That I have been a witness to. When Mr. Gott was working long hours, I was then watching upon the premises; I used to go through the mills, and I have seen some slubbers encouraging them to sing hymns in order to keep awake; others would be beating them about, and throwing things at them to keep them awake.

When a child gets 3 s. a week, does that go much toward its subsistence? — No, it will not keep it as it should.

When they got 6 s. or 7 s. when they were pieceners, if they reduced the hours of labour, would they not get less?—They would get a halpenny a day less, but I would rather have less wages and less work.

Do you receive any parish assistance? — No.

Why do you allow your children to go to those places where they are overworked? — Necessity compels a man that has children to let them work.

Mr. Matthew Crabtree, called in; and examined

What age are you? — Twenty-two.

What is your occupation? — A blanket manufacturer.

Have you ever been employed in a factory? — Yes.

At what age did you first go to work in one? — Eight.

How long did you continue in that occupation? — Four years.

Will you state the hours of labour at the period when you first went to the factory, in ordinary times? — From 6 in the morning to 8 at night.

Fourteen hours? — Yes.

With what intervals for refreshment and rest? — An hour at noon.

Then you had no resting time allowed in which to take your breakfast, or what is in Yorkshire called your "drinking"? — No.

When the trade was brisk what were your hours? — From 5 in the morning to 9 in the evening.

Sixteen hours? —Yes.

With what intervals at dinner? — An hour.

How far did you live from the mill? — About two miles.

Was there any time allowed for you to get your breakfast in the mill? — No.

Did you take it before you left home? — Generally.

During those long hours of labour could you be punctual; how did you awake? — I seldom did awake spontaneously; I was most generally awoke or lifted out of bed, sometimes asleep, by my parents.

Were you always in time? — No.

What was the consequence if you had been too late? — I was most commonly beaten.

Severely? — Yes severely, I thought.

Will you state the effect that those long hours had upon the state of your health and feelings? — I was, when working those long hours commonly much fatigued at night, when I left my work; so much so that I sometimes should have slept as I walked if I had not stumbled and started awake again; and so sick often that I could not eat, and what I did eat I vomited.

Did the labour spoil your appetite? — It did.

In what situation were you in the mill? — I was a piecener.

Will you state for this Committee whether piecening is a very laborious employment for children or not? — It is a very laborious employment. Pieceners are continually running to and fro, and on their feet the whole day.

The duty of the piecener is to take the cardings from one part of the machinery and placed them on another? — Yes. So that the labour is not only continual, but is unabated to the last? — It is unabated to the last.

Do you not think, from your own experience, that the speed of the machinery is so calculated as to demand the utmost exertions of a child, supposing the hours were moderate? — It is as much as they can do when they are not very much fatigued to keep up with their work, and towards the close of the day, when they came to be more fatigued, they cannot keep up with it very well, and the consequence is that they are beaten to spur them on.

Peter Smart, *called in; and examined*

Where do you reside? — At Dundee.

Have you worked in a mill from your youth? — Yes, since I was 5 years of age.

Had you a father and mother in the country at the time? — My mother stopped in Perth, about eleven miles from the mill, and my father was in the army.

Were you hired for any length of time when you went? — Yes, my mother got 15 s. for six years, I having my meat and clothes.

What were your hours of labour, as you recollect, in the mill? — In the summer season we were very scarce of water.

But when you had sufficient water, how long did you work? —We began at 4-o-clock in the morning and worked till 10 or 11 at night; as long as we could stand on our feet.

Were you kept on the premises constantly? — Constantly.

Locked up? — Yes, locked up.

Night and day? — Night and day; I never went home while I was at the mill.

Do the children ever attempt to run away? — Very often.

Were they pursued and brought back again? — Yes, the overseer pursued them and brought them back.

Did you ever attempt to run away? — Yes, I ran away twice.

And you were brought back? — Yes; and I was sent up to the master's loft, and thrashed with a whip for running away.

Do you know whether the children were, in point of fact, compelled to stop during the whole time for which they were engaged? — Yes, they were.

By law? — I cannot say by law; but they were compelled by the master; I never saw any law used there but the law of their own hands. . . .

TESTIMONY GATHERED BY THE ASHLEY MINES COMMISSION
(1842)

Thomas Dunn, Esq. *Chief Manager*

Believes that morals of the collier's children are decidedly better than those of the Sheffield artizans, who are generally bad enough in Sheffield though not so bad as in Manchester; thinks education among colliers' children to be very much neglected;

though he thinks they will generally be able to read; they are usually employed at early ages in opening doors, but this prevents any further education on week days after they go into the pits; believes no girls are employed close to Sheffield in coal pits, but at other places is aware that girls are worked naked down to their waists the same as men; has no objection to an Act preventing the employment of children in coal pits before they are 11 years old; it would be no injury to their trade, but might be hard upon the poor parents; the hours which they work are maximum 12, and minimum 10.

Payne, Esq. coal master

That children are employed generally at nine years old in the coal pits and sometimes at eight. In fact, the smaller the vein of coal is in height, the younger and smaller are the children required; the work occupies from six to seven hours per day in the pits; they are not ill-used or worked beyond their strength; a good deal of depravity exists but they are certainly not worse in morals than in other branches of the Sheffield trade, but upon the whole superior; the morals of this district are materially improving; Mr. Bruce, the clergyman, has been zealous and active in endeavoring to ameliorate their moral and religious education. . . .

Ann Eggley, hurrier in Messrs. Thorpe's colliery. 18 years old:

I'm sure I don't know how to spell my name. We go at four in the morning, and sometimes at half-past four. We begin to work as soon as we get down. We get out after four, sometimes at five, in the evening. We work the whole time except an hour for dinner, and sometimes we haven't time to eat. I hurry by myself, and have done so for long. I know the corves are very heavy, they are the biggest corves anywhere about. The work is far too hard for me; the sweat runs off me all over sometimes. I am very tired at night. Sometimes when we get home at night we have not power to wash us, and then we go to bed. Sometimes we fall asleep in the chair. Father said last night it was both a shame and a disgrace for girls to work as we do, but there was naught else for us to do. I began to hurry when I was seven and I have been hurrying ever since. I have been 11 years in the pits. The girls are always tired. I was poorly twice this winter; it was with headache. I hurry for Robert Wiggins; he is not akin to me. . . . We don't always get enough to eat and drink, but we get a good supper. I have known my father go at two in

the morning to work . . . and he didn't come out till four. I am quite sure that we work constantly 12 hours except on Saturdays. We wear trousers and our shifts in the pit and great big shoes clinkered and nailed. The girls never work naked to the waist in our pit. The men don't insult us in the pit. The conduct of the girls in the pit is good enough sometimes and sometimes bad enough. I never went to a day-school. I went a little to a Sunday-school, but I soon gave it over. I thought it too bad to be confined both Sundays and week-days. I walk about and get the fresh air on Sundays. I have not learnt to read. I don't know my letters. I never learnt naught. I never go to church or chapel; there is no church or chapel at Gawber, there is none nearer than a mile. . . . I have never heard that a good man came into the world who was God's son to save sinners. I never heard of Christ at all. Nobody has ever told me about him, nor have my father and mother ever taught me to pray. I know no prayer: I never pray.

Patience Kershaw, aged 17:

My father has been dead about a year; my mother is living and has ten children, five lads and five lasses; the oldest is about thirty, the youngest is four; three lasses go to mill; all the lads are colliers, two getters and three hurriers; one lives at home and does nothing; mother does nought but look after home.

All my sisters have been hurriers, but three went to the mill. Alice went because her legs swelled from hurrying in cold water when she was hot. I never went to day-school; I go to Sunday-school, but I cannot read or write; I go to pit at five o'clock in the morning and come out at five in the evening; I get my breakfast of porridge and milk first; I take my dinner with me, a cake, and eat it as I go; I do not stop or rest any time for the purpose; I get nothing else until I get home, and then have potatoes and meat, not every day meat. I hurry in the clothes I have now got on, trousers and ragged jacket; the bald place upon my head is made by thrusting the corves; my legs have never swelled, but sisters' did when they went to mill; I hurry the corves a mile and more under ground and back; they weigh 300 cwt.; I hurry 11 a-day; I wear a belt and chain at the workings to get the corves out; the putters that I work for are *naked* except their caps; they pull off all their clothes; I see them at work when I go up; sometimes they beat me, if I am not quick enough, with their hands; they strike me upon my back; the boys take liberties with me, sometimes, they pull me about; I am the only girl in the pit; there are about 20 boys and 15 men; all the men are naked; I would rather work in mill than in coal-pit.

Isabel Wilson, 38 years old, coal putter:

When women have children thick (fast) they are compelled to take them down early. I have been married 19 years and have had 10 bairns; seven are in life. When on Sir John's work was a carrier of coals, which caused me to miscarry five times from the strains, and was gai ill after each. Putting is no so oppressive; last child was born on Saturday morning, and I was at work on the Friday night.

Once met with an accident; a coal brake my cheek-bone, which kept me idle some weeks.

I have wrought below 30 years, and so has the guid man; he is getting touched in the breath now.

None of the children read, as the work is no regular. I did read once, but no able to atten to it now; when I go below lassie 10 years of age keeps house and makes the broth or stir-about.

(Nine sleep in two bedsteads; there did not appear to be any beds, and the whole of the furniture consisted of two chairs, three stools, at table, a kail-pot and a few broken basins and cups. Upon asking if the furniture was all they had, the guid wife said, furniture was of no use, as it was so troublesome to flit with.)

THOMAS CARLYLE (1795-1881)

The son of a humble Scottish stonemason, Thomas Carlyle died in London one of the most famous men of letters in the English speaking world. His life spanned nearly the whole of the nineteenth century. Born in 1795 in the midst of the French Revolutionary era, he lived to see the transformation of the British Isles into the industrial workshop of the world and the triumph of liberal democracy. For all these events he expressed an intense and vocal dislike. The first of his books to bring him fame, *The French Revolution, a History* (1837) is a classic of historical writing, but it is also a moral Philippic against revolution. It was followed by lives of Cromwell and Frederick the Great, massive historical biographies in which he gave full rein to his passion for military history and hero worship. *Past and Present* (1843), written in the midst of the "wretched thirties" and "hungry forties," was his commentary on the blessings of industrialism. Although outside the main stream of nineteenth century thought, no other Victorian writer had the popular appeal of this stern, Old-Testament prophet.

The following selections are from the original 1843 edition of *Past and Present*.

PAST AND PRESENT (1843)

Ernst ist das Leben.—Schiller

Book I

PROEM

CHAPTER I

MIDAS

The condition of England, on which many pamphlets are now in the course of publication, and many thoughts unpublished are going on in every reflective head, is justly regarded as one of the most ominous, and withal one of the strangest, ever seen in this world. England is full of wealth, of multifarious produce, supply for human want in every kind; yet England is dying of inanition. With unabated bounty the land of England blooms and grows; waving with yellow harvests; thick-studded with workshops, industrial implements, with fifteen millions of workers, understood to be the strongest, the cunningest and the willingest our Earth ever had; these men are here; the work they have done; the fruit they have realized is here, abundant, exuberant on every hand of us: and behold, some baleful fiat as of Enchantment has gone forth, saying, "Touch it not, ye workers, ye master-workers, ye master-idlers; none of you can touch it, no man of you shall be the better for it; this is enchanted fruit!" On the poor workers such fiat falls first, in its rudest shape; but on the rich master-workers too it falls; neither can the rich master-idlers, nor any richest or highest man escape; but all are like to be brought low with it and made "poor" enough, in the money sense or a far fataler one.

Of these successful skilful workers some two millions, it is now counted, sit in Workhouses, Poorlaw Prisons; or have "outdoor relief" flung over the wall to them,—the workhouse Bastille being filled to bursting, and the strong Poor-law broken asunder by a stronger. They sit there, these many months now; their hope of deliverance as yet small. In workhouses, pleasantly so-named, because work cannot be done in them. Twelve-hundred-thousand workers in England alone; their cunning right-hand lamed, lying idle in their sorrowful bosom; their hopes, outlooks, share of this fair world, shut-in by narrow walls. They sit there, pent up, as in a kind of horrid enchantment; glad to be imprisoned and enchanted, that they may not perish starved. The picturesque Tourist, in a sunny autumn day, through this bounteous realm of England, descries the Union Workhouse on his path.

Passing by the Workhouse of St. Ives in Huntingdonshire, on a bright day last autumn (says the picturesque Tourist), I saw sitting on wooden benches, in front of their Bastille and within their ring-wall and its railings, some half-hundred or more of these men. Tall robust figures, young mostly or of middle age; of honest countenance, many of them thoughtful and even intelligent-looking men. They sat there, near by one another; but in a kind of torpor, especially in a silence, which was very striking. In silence: for, alas, what word was to be said? An Earth all lying round, crying, Come and till me, come and reap me;—yet we here sit enchanted! In the eyes and brows of these men hung the gloomiest expression, not of anger, but of grief and shame and manifold inarticulate distress and weariness; they returned my glance with a glance that seemed to say, "Do not look at us. We sit enchanted here, we know not why. The Sun shines and the Earth calls; and, by the governing Powers and Impotences of this England, we are forbidden to obey. It is impossible, they tell us!" There was something that reminded me of Dante's Hell in the look of all this; and I rode swiftly away. . . .

Descend where you will into the lower class, in Town or Country, by what avenue you will, by Factory Inquiries, Agricultural Inquiries, by Revenue Returns, by Mining-Laborer Committees, by opening your own eyes and looking, the same sorrowful result discloses itself: you have to admit that the working body of this rich English Nation has sunk or is fast sinking into a state, to which, all sides of it considered, there was literally never any parallel. . . .

. . . This successful industry of England, with its plethoric wealth, has as yet made nobody rich; it is an enchanted wealth, and belongs yet to nobody. We might ask, Which of us has it enriched? We can spend thousands where we once spent hundreds; but can purchase nothing good with them. In Poor and Rich, instead of noble thrift and plenty, there is idle luxury alternating with mean scarcity and inability. We have sumptuous garnitures for our Life, but have forgotten to *live* in the middle of them. It is an enchanted wealth; no man of us can yet touch it. The class of men who feel that they are truly better off by means of it, let them give us their name!

Many men eat finer cookery, drink dearer liquors,—with what advantage they can report, and their Doctors can: but in the heart of them, if we go out of the dyspeptic stomach, what increase of blessedness is there? Are they better, beautifuler, stronger, braver? Are they even what they call "happier"? Do they look with satisfaction on more things and human faces in this God's-Earth; do more things and human faces look with satisfaction on them? Not so. Human faces gloom discordantly, disloyally on one another. Things, if it be not mere cotton and iron things, are growing disobedient to man. The Master Worker is enchanted, for the present, like his Workhouse Workman; clamours in vain hitherto, for a very simple sort of "Liberty": the liberty "to buy where he finds it cheapest, to sell where he finds it dearest." With guineas jingling in every pocket, he was no whit richer; but now, the very guineas threatening to vanish, he feels that he is poor indeed. Poor Master Worker! And the Master Unworker, is not he in a still fataler situation? Pausing amid his game-preserves, with awful eye,—as he well may! Coercing fifty-pound tenants; coercing, bribing, cajoling: "doing what he likes with his own." His mouth full of loud futilities, and arguments to prove the excellence of his Corn-law; and in his heart the blackest misgiving, a desperate half-consciousness that his excellent Corn-law is *in*defensible, that his loud arguments for it are of a kind to strike men too literally *dumb*.

To whom, then, is this wealth of England wealth? Who is it that it blesses; makes happier, wiser, beautifuler, in any way better? Who has got hold of it, to make it fetch and carry for him, like a true servant, not like a false mock-servant; to do him any real service whatsoever? As yet no one. We have more riches than any Nation ever had before; we have less good of them than any Nation ever had before. Our successful industry is hitherto unsuccessful; a strange success, if we stop here! In the midst of plethoric plenty, the people perish; with gold walls, and full barns, no man feels himself safe or satisfied. Workers, Master Workers, Unworkers, all men, come to a pause; stand fixed, and cannot farther. Fatal paralysis spreading inwards, from the extremities, in St. Ives workhouses, in Stockport cellars, through all limbs, as if towards the heart itself. Have we actually got enchanted, then; accursed by some god?—

Midas longed for gold, and insulted the Olympians. He got gold, so that whatsoever he touched became gold,—and he, with his long ears, was little the better for it. Midas had misjudged the celestial music-tones; Midas had insulted Apollo and the gods: the gods gave him his wish, and a pair of long ears, which also were a good appendage to it. What a truth in these old Fables!

CHAPTER II
THE SPHINX

The secret of gold, Midas, which he with his long ears never could discover, was, that he had offended the Supreme Powers;—that he had parted company with the eternal inner Facts of this Universe, and followed the transient outer Appearances thereof; and so was arrived *here*. Properly it is the secret of all unhappy men and unhappy nations. Had they known Nature's right truth, Nature's right truth would have made them free. They have become enchanted; stagger spell-bound, reeling on the brink of huge peril, because they were not wise enough. They have forgotten the right Inner True, and taken up the Outer Sham-true. . . .

Foolish men imagine that because judgment for an evil thing is delayed, there is no justice, but an accidental one, here below. Judgment for an evil thing is many times delayed some day or two, some century or two, but it is sure as life, it is sure as death! In the centre of the world-whirlwind, verily now as in the oldest days, dwells and speaks a God. The great soul of the world is *just*. O Brother, can it be needful now, at this late epoch of experience, after eighteen centuries of Christian preaching for one thing, to remind thee of such a fact; which all manner of Mahometans, old Pagan Romans, Jews, Scythians and heathen Greeks, and indeed more or less all men that God made, have managed at one time to see into; nay which thou thyself, till "redtape" strangled the inner life of thee, hadst once some inkling of: That there *is* justice here below; and even, at bottom, that there is nothing else but justice. . . .

CHAPTER III

MANCHESTER INSURRECTION

. . . Unhappy Workers, unhappier Idlers, unhappy men and women of this actual England. We are yet very far from an answer, and there will be no existence for us without finding one. "A fair day's-wages for a fair day's-work": it is as just a demand as Governed men ever made of Governing. It is the everlasting right of man. Indisputable as Gospels, as arithmetical multiplication-tables: it must and will have itself fulfilled;—and yet, in these times of ours, with what enormous difficulty, nextdoor to impossibility! For the times are really strange; of a complexity intricate with all the new width of the ever-widening world; times here of half-frantic velocity of impetus, there of the deadest-looking stillness and paralysis; times definable as showing two qualities, Dilettantism and Mammonism;—most intricate obstructed times! Nay, if there were not a Heaven's radiance of Justice, prophetic, clearly of Heaven, discernible behind all these confused world-wide entanglements, of Landlord interests, Manufacturing interests, Tory-Whig interests, and who knows what other interests, expediencies, vested interests, established possessions, inveterate Dilettantisms, Midas-eared Mammonisms,—it would seem to every one a flat impossibility, which all wise men might as well at once abandon. If you do not know eternal Justice from momentary Expediency, . . . you also would talk of impossibility! But it is only difficult, it is not impossible. Possible? It is, with whatever difficulty, very clearly inevitable. . . .

Shall we say then, the world has retrograded in its talent of apportioning wages to work, in late days? The world had always a talent of that sort, better or worse. Time was when the mere *hand*worker needed not announce his claim to the world by Manchester Insurrections!—The world, with its Wealth of Nations, supply-and-demand and suchlike, has of late days been terribly inattentive to that question of work and wages. We will not say, the poor world has retrograded even here: we will say rather, the world has been rushing on with such fiery animation to get work and ever more work done, it has had no time to think of dividing the wages; and has merely left them to be scrambled for by the Law of the Stronger, Law of Supply-and-demand, law of Laissez-faire, and other idle Laws and Un-laws,—saying, in its dire haste to get the work done, that is well enough!

And now the world will have to pause a little, and take up that other side of the problem, and in right earnest strive for some solution of that. For it has become pressing. What is the use of your spun shirts? They hang there by the million unsaleable; and here, by the million, are diligent bare backs that can get no hold of them. Shirts are useful for covering human backs; useless otherwise, an unbearable mockery otherwise. You have fallen terribly behind with that side of the problem! Manchester Insurrections, French Revolutions, and thousandfold phenomena great and small, announce loudly that you must bring it forward a little again. Never till now, in the history of an Earth which to this hour nowhere refuses to grow corn if you will plough it, to yield shirts if you will spin and weave in it, did the mere manual two-handed worker (however it might fare with other workers) cry in vain for such "wages" as *he* means by "fair wages," namely food and warmth! The Godlike could not and cannot be paid; but the Earthly always could. Gurth, a mere swineherd, born thrall of Cedric the Saxon, tended pigs in the wood, and did get some parings of the pork. Why, the four-footed worker has already *got* all that this two-handed one is clamoring for! How often must I remind you? There is not a horse in England, able and willing to work, but *has* due food and lodging; and goes about sleek-coated, satisfied in heart. . . . We pray you, let the word *impossible* disappear from your vocabulary in this matter. It is of awful omen; to all of us, and to yourselves first of all.

CHAPTER IV

MORRISON'S PILL

What is to be done, what would you have us do? asks many a one with a tone of impatience, almost of reproach; and then, if you mention some one thing, some two things, twenty things that might be done, turns round with a satirical tehee, and "These are your remedies!" The state of mind indicated by such question, and such rejoinder, is worth reflecting on.

It seems to be taken for granted, by these interrogative philosophers, that there is some "thing," or handful of "things," which could be done; some Act of Parliament, "remedial measure" or the like, which could be passed, whereby the social malady were fairly fronted, conquered, put an end to; so that, with your remedial measure in your pocket, you could then go on triumphant, and be troubled no farther. "You tell us the evil," cry such persons, as if justly aggrieved, "and do not tell us how it is to be cured!"

How it is to be cured? Brothers, I am sorry I have got no Morrison's Pill for curing the maladies of Society. It were infinitely handier if we had a Morrison's Pill, Act of Parliament, or remedial measure, which men could swallow, one good time, and then go on in their old courses, cleared from all miseries and mischiefs! Unluckily we have none such; unluckily the Heavens themselves, in their rich pharmacopoeia, contain none such. There will no "thing" be done that will cure you. . . . Not Emigration, Education, Corn-Law Abrogation, Sanitary Regulation, Land Property-Tax; not these alone, nor a thousand times as much as these. . . . Alas, by no Reform Bill, Ballot-box, Five-point Charter, by no boxes or bills or charters, can you perform this alchemy: "Given a world of Knaves, to produce an Honesty from their united action!" It is a distillation, once for all, not possible. You pass it through alembic after alembic, it comes out still a Dishonesty, with a new dress on it, a new colour to it. "While we ourselves continue valets, how *can* any hero come to govern us?" We are governed, very infallibly, by the "sham-hero,"—whose name is Quack. . . . Not any universal Morrison's Pill shall we then, either as swallowers or as vendors, ask after at all; but a far different sort of remedies: Quacks shall no more have dominion over us, but true Heroes and Healers. . . .

98

Chapter V
ARISTOCRACY OF TALENT

We must have more Wisdom to govern us, we must be governed by the Wisest, we must have an Aristocracy of Talent! cry many. True, most true; but how to get it? The following extract from our young friend of the *Houndsditch Indicator* is worth perusing: "At this time," says he, "while there is a cry everywhere, articulate or inarticulate, for an 'Aristocracy of Talent,' a Governing Class namely which did govern, not merely which took the wages of governing . . . it may not be altogether useless to remind some of the greener-headed sort what a dreadfully difficult affair the getting of such an Aristocracy is. . . ."

"For example, you Bobus Higgins, Sausagemaker on the great scale, who are raising such a clamour for this Aristocracy of Talent, what is it that you do, in that big heart of yours, chiefly in very fact pay reverence to? Is it to talent, intrinsic manly worth of any kind, you unfortunate Bobus? The manliest man that you saw going in a ragged coat, did you ever reverence him; did you so much as know that he was a manly man at all, till his coat grew better? Talent! I understand you to be able to worship the fame of talent, the power, cash, celebrity or other success of talent; but the talent itself is a thing you never saw with eyes. Nay, what is it in yourself that you are proudest of, that you take most pleasure in surveying meditatively in thoughtful moments? Speak now, is it the bare Bobus stript of his very name and shirt, and turned loose upon society, that you admire and thank Heaven for; or Bobus with his cash-accounts and larders dropping fatness, with his respectabilities, warm garnitures, and pony-chaise, admirable in some measure to certain of the flunky species? . . . Bobus, you are in a vicious circle, rounder than one of your own sausages; and will never vote for or promote any talent, except what talent or sham-talent has already *got* itself voted for!"—We here cut short the *Indicator*; . . .

Our "Aristocracy of Talent" seems at a considerable distance yet; does it not, O Bobus?

(The next two chapters from Book II require a word of explanation. When writing Book II, the "Past" of *Past and Present,* Carlyle had at hand a recently published Latin manuscript, Jocelin of Brakelond's account of the life of a Medieval monk, Samson of Norfolk. Carlyle uses the chron-

icle (he calls Jocelin his Boswell) to contrast the values
of the twelfth century with the "condition of England"
of his own age, not in a romantic effort to return to the
past but to recapture the spiritual vigor of Abbot Samson
and the dignity of labor.)

Book II
THE ANCIENT MONK
CHAPTER V
TWELFTH CENTURY

Dim, as through a long vista of seven centuries, dim and
very strange looks that monk-life to us; the ever surprising circumstance this. That it is a *fact* and no dream, that we see it
there, and gaze into the very eyes of it! Smoke rises daily from
those culinary chimney throats; there are living human beings
there, who chant, loud-braying, their matins, nones, vespers; awak-
ening *echoes,* not to the bodily ear alone. St. Edmund's Shrine,
perpetually illuminated, glows ruddy through the night, and
through the night of centuries withal. . . .

How much is still alive in England; how much has not yet
come to life! A Feudal Aristocracy is still alive, in the prime of
life, superintending the cultivation of the land, and less consciously the distribution of the produce of the land, the adjust-
ment of the quarrels of the land; judging, soldiering, adjusting;
everywhere governing the people,—so that even a Gurth, born
thrall of Cedric, lacks not his due parings of the pigs he tends.
Governing;—and, alas, also game-preserving; so that a Robin
Hood, a William Scarlet and others have, in these days, put on
Lincoln coats, and taken to living, in some universal-suffrage manner, under the greenwood tree!

How silent, on the other hand, lie all cotton-trades and
suchlike; not a steeple-chimney yet got on from sea to sea!
North of the Humber, a stern Willemus Conquaestor burnt the
Country, finding it unruly, into very stern repose. Wild fowl
scream in those ancient silences, wild cattle roam in those ancient
solitudes; the scanty sulky Norse-bred population all coerced into
silence,—feeling that, under these new Norman Governors, their
history has probably as good as *ended*. Men and Northumbrian
Norse populations know little what has ended, what is but beginning! The Ribble and the Aire roll down, as yet unpolluted
by dyers' chemistry; tenanted by merry trouts and piscatory ot-

ters; the sunbeam and the vacant wind's-blast alone traversing those moors. Side by side sleep the coal-strata and the iron-strata for so many ages; no steam-demon has yet risen smoking into being. Saint Mungo rules in Glasgow; James Watt still slumbering in the deep of Time. *Mancunium,* Manceaster, what we now call Manchester, spins no cotton,—if it be not *wool* 'cottons,' clipped from the backs of mountain sheep. . . . The centuries are big; and the birth-hour is coming, not yet come. . . .

CHAPTER XVII
THE BEGINNINGS

It is all work and forgotten work, this peopled, clothed, articulate-speaking, high-towered, wide-acred world. The hands of forgotten brave men have made it a World for us;—they,— honour to them, they, in *spite* of the idle and the dastard. This English Land, here and now, is the summary of what was found of wise and noble, and accordant with God's truth, in all the generations of English Men. Our English Speech is speakable because there were Hero-Poets of our blood and lineage; speakable in proportion to the number of these. This Land of England has its conquerors, possessors, which change from epoch to epoch, from day to day; but its real conquerors, creators, and eternal proprietors are these following, and their representatives if you can find them: All the Heroic Souls that ever were in England, each in their degree; all the men that ever cut a thistle, drained a puddle out of England, contrived a wise scheme in England, did or said a true and valiant thing in England. I tell thee, they had not a hammer to begin with; and yet Wren built St. Paul's: not an articulated syllable; and yet there have come English Literatures, Elizabethan Literatures, . . . and other Literatures. . . .

Book III
The Modern Worker
CHAPTER I
PHENOMENA

But, it is said, our religion is gone: we no longer believe in St. Edmund, no longer see the figure of him "on the rim of the sky," . . .

It is even so. To speak in the ancient dialect, we "have forgotten God";—in the most modern dialect and very truth of the matter, we have taken up the Fact of this Universe as it *is not*. We have quietly closed our eyes to the eternal Substance of things, and opened them only to the Shows and Shams of things. We quietly believe this Universe to be intrinsically a great unintelligible PERHAPS; extrinsically, clear enough, it is a great, most extensive Cattlefold and Workhouse, with most extensive Kitchen-ranges, Dining-tables,—whereat he is wise who can find a place! All the Truth of this Universe is uncertain; only the profit and loss of it, the pudding and praise of it, are and remain very visible to the practical man.

There is no longer any God for us! God's Laws are become a Greatest-Happiness Principle, a Parliamentary Expediency: the Heavens overarch us only as an Astronomical Timekeeper; a butt for Herschel-telescopes to shoot science at, to shoot sentimentalities at:—in our and old Jonson's dialect, man has lost the *soul* out of him; and now, after the due period,— begins to find the want of it! This is verily the plague-spot; centre of the universal Social Gangrene, threatening all modern things with frightful death. . . There is no religion; there is no God; man has lost his soul, and vainly seeks antiseptic salt. Vainly: in killing Kings, in passing Reform Bills, in French Revolutions, Manchester Insurrections, is found no remedy. . . .

For actually this is *not* the real fact of the world; the world is not made so, but otherwise!—Truly, any Society setting out from this No-God hypothesis will arrive at a result or two. . . .

Nature's Laws, I must repeat, are eternal: her small still voice, speaking from the inmost heart of us, shall not, under terrible penalties be disregarded. No one man can depart from the truth without damage to himself; no one million of men; no Twenty-seven Millions of men. Show me a Nation fallen everywhere into this course, so that each expects it, permits it to others and himself, I will show you a Nation travelling with one assent on the broad way. The broad way, however many Banks of England, Cotton-Mills and Duke's Palaces it may have. Not at happy Elysian fields, and everlasting crowns of victory, earned by silent Valour, will this Nation arrive; but at precipices, devouring gulfs, if it pause not. Nature has appointed happy fields, victorious laurel-crowns; but only to the brave and true: *Un*nature, what we call Chaos, holds nothing in it but vacuities, devouring gulfs. What are Twenty-seven Millions, and their unanimity? Believe them not: the Worlds and the Ages, God and Nature and All Men say otherwise. . . .

Oh, it is frightful when a whole Nation, as our Fathers used to say, has "forgotten God"; has remembered only Mammon, and what Mammon leads to! When your self-trumpeting Hatmaker is the emblem of almost all makers, and workers, and men, that make anything,—from soul-overseerships, body-overseerships, epic poems, acts of parliament, to hats and shoe-blacking! Not one false man but does uncountable mischief: how much, in a generation or two, will Twenty-seven Millions, mostly false, manage to accumulate? The sum of it, visible in every street, market-place, senate-house, circulating library, cathedral, cotton-mill, and union-workhouse, fills one *not* with a comic feeling!

CHAPTER II

GOSPEL OF MAMMONISM

True, it must be owned, we for the present, with our Mammon-Gospel, have come to strange conclusions. We call it a Society; and go about professing openly the totalest separation, isolation. Our life is not a mutual helpfulness; but rather, cloaked under due laws-of-war, named "fair competition" and so forth, it is a mutual hostility. We have profoundly forgotten everywhere that *Cash-payment* is not the sole relation of human beings; we think, nothing doubting, that *it* absolves and liquidates all engagements of man. "My starving workers?" answers the rich mill-owner: "Did not I hire them fairly in the market? Did I not pay them, to the last sixpence, the sum covenanted for? What have I to do with them more?"—Verily Mammon-worship is a melancholy creed. When Cain, for his own behoof, had killed Abel, and was questioned, "Where is thy brother?" he too made answer, "Am I my brother's keeper?" Did I not pay my brother *his* wages, the thing he had merited from me?

O sumptuous Merchant-Prince, illustrious game-preserving Duke, is there no way of 'killing' thy brother but Cain's rude way! 'A good man by the very look of him, by his very presence with us as a fellow wayfarer in this Life-pilgrimage, *promises* so much:' wo to him if he forget all such promises, if he never know that they were given! To a deadened soul, seared with the brute Idolatry of Sense, to whom going to Hell is equivalent to not making money, all 'promises,' and moral duties, that cannot be pleaded for in Courts of Requests, address themselves in vain. Money he can be ordered to pay, but nothing more. I have not heard in all Past History, and expect not to hear in all Future History, of any Society anywhere under God's Heaven supporting itself on such Philosophy. The Universe is not made so; it is made otherwise than so. The man or nation of men that thinks it is made so, marches forward nothing doubting, step after step; but marches—whither we know! ...

One of Dr. Alison's Scotch facts struck us much. A poor Irish Widow, her husband having died in one of the Lanes of Edinburgh, went forth with her three children, bare of all resource, to solicit help from the Charitable Establishments of that City. At this Charitable Establishment and then at that she was refused; referred from one to the other, helped by none;—till she had exhausted them all; till her strength and heart failed her: she sank down in typhus-fever; died, and infected her Lane with fever, so that "seventeen other persons" died of fever there in consequence. The humane Physician asks thereupon, as with a heart too full for speaking, Would it not have been *economy* to help this poor Widow? She took typhus-fever, and killed seventeen of you!—Very curious. The forlorn Irish Widow applies to her fellow-creatures, as if saying, "Behold I am sinking, bare of help: ye must help me! I am your sister, bone of your bone; one God made us: ye must help me!" They answer, "No, impossible; thou art no sister of ours." But she proves her sisterhood; her typhus-fever kills *them*: they actually were her brothers, though denying it! Had human creature ever to go lower for a proof? ...

"Impossible": of a certain two-legged animal with feathers it is said, if you draw a distinct chalk-circle round him, he sits imprisoned, as if girt with the iron ring of Fate; and will die there, though within sight of victuals,—or sit in sick misery there, and be fatted to death. The name of this poor two-legged animal is—Goose; and they make of him, when well fattened, *Pate de foie gras,* much prized by some!

Chapter III
GOSPEL OF DILETTANTISM

But after all, the Gospel of Dilettantism, producing a Governing Class who do not govern, nor understand in the least that they are bound or expected to govern, is still mournfuler than that of Mammonism. Mammonism, as we said, at least works; this goes idle. Mammonism has seized some portion of the message of Nature to man; and seizing that, and following it, will seize and appropriate more and more of Nature's message: but Dilettantism has missed it wholly. "Make money;" that will mean withal, "Do work in order to make money." But, "Go gracefully idle in Mayfair," what does or can that mean? An idle, game-preserving and even corn-lawing Aristocracy, in such an England as ours: has the world, if we take thought of it, ever seen such a phenomenon till very lately? Can it long continue to see such? . . .

CHAPTER IV

HAPPY

Does not the whole wretchedness, the whole *Atheism* as I call it, of man's ways, in these generations, shadow itself for us in that unspeakable Life-philosophy of his: the pretension to be what he calls "happy"? Every pitifulest whipster that walks within a skin has his head filled with the notion that he is, shall be, or by all human and divine laws ought to be "happy." His wishes, the pitifulest whipster's, are to be fulfilled for him; his days, the pitifulest whipster's, are to flow on in ever-gentle current of enjoyment, impossible even for the gods. The prophets preach to us, Thou shalt be happy; thou shalt love pleasant things, and find them. The people clamor, Why have we not found pleasant things?

We construct our theory of Human Duties, not on any Greatest-Nobleness Principle, never so mistaken; no, but on a Greatest-Happiness Principle. "The word *Soul* with us, as in some Slavonic dialects, seems to be synonymous with *Stomach*." We plead and speak, in our Parliaments and elsewhere, not as from the Soul, but from the Stomach;—wherefore indeed our pleadings are so slow to profit. We plead not for God's Justice; we are not ashamed to stand clamoring and pleading for our own "interests," our own rents and trade-profits. . . .

"Happy," my brother? First of all, what difference is it whether thou art happy or not! Today becomes Yesterday so fast, all Tomorrows become Yesterdays; and there is no question whatever of the "happiness" but quite another question. . . .

The only happiness a brave man ever troubled himself with asking much about was, happiness enough to get his work done. Not "I can't eat!" but "I can't work!" that was the burden of all wise complaining among men. It is, after all, the one unhappiness of a man. That he cannot work; that he cannot get his destiny as a man fulfilled. Behold, the day is passing swiftly over, our life is passing swiftly over; and the night cometh when no man can work. The night once come, our happiness, our unhappiness,—it is all abolished; vanished, clean gone; a thing that has been: "not of the slightest consequence" whether we were happy as eupeptic Curtis, as the fattest pig of Epicurus, or unhappy as Job with potsherds, as musical Byron with Giaours and sensibilities of the heart; as the unmusical Meat-jack with hard labour and rust! But our work,—behold that is not abolished, that has not vanished: our work, behold it remains, or the want of it remains;—for endless Times and Eternities, remains; and that is now the sole question with us forevermore! . . . Happiness, unhappiness: all that was but the *wages* thou hadst. . . . Where is thy work? Swift, out with it, let us see they work! . . .

CHAPTER VII

OVER-PRODUCTION

But what reflective readers say of a Governing Class, such as ours, addressing its Workers with an indictment of "Over-Production"! Over-production: runs it not so? "Ye miscellaneous, ignoble manufacturing individuals, ye have produced too much! We accuse you of making above two-hundred thousand shirts for the bare backs of mankind. Your trousers too, which you have made, of fustian, of cassimere, of Scotch-plaid, of jane, nankeen and woolen broadcloth, are they not manifold? Of hats for the human head, of shoes for the human foot, of stools to sit on, spoons to eat with—Nay, what say we hats or shoes? You produce gold-watches, jewelries, silver-forks, and epergnes, commodes, chiffoniers, stuffed sofas—Heavens, the Commercial Bazaar and multitudinous Howel-and-Jameses cannot contain you. You have produced, produced;—he that seeks your indictment, let him look around. Millions of shirts, and empty pairs of breeches, hang there in judgment against you. We accuse you of over-producing: you are criminally guilty of producing shirts, breeches, hats, shoes and commodities, in a frightful over-abundance. And now there is a glut, and your operatives cannot be fed!"

Never surely, against an earnest Working Mammonism was there brought, by Game-preserving aristrocratic Dilettantism, a stranger accusation, since this world began. My lords and gentlemen,—why, it was *you* that were appointed, by the fact and by the theory of your position on the Earth, to "make and administer Laws,"—that is to say, in a world such as ours, to guard against "gluts"; against honest operatives, who had done their work, remaining unfed! I say, *you* were appointed to preside over the Distribution and Apportionment of the Wages of Work done; and to see well that there went no labourer without his hire, were it of money-coins, were it of hemp gallows-ropes: that function was yours, and from immemorial time has been yours, and as yet no other's. These poor shirt-spinners have forgotten much, which by the virtual unwritten law of their position they should have remembered: but by any written recognised law of their position, what have they forgotten? They were set to make shirts. The Community with all its voices commanded them, saying, "Make shirts;"—and there the shirts are! Too many shirts? Well, that is a novelty, in this intemperate Earth, with its nine-hundred millions of bare backs! But the Community commanded you, saying, "See that the shirts are well apportioned, that our Human Laws be emblem of God's Laws;"—and where is the apportionment? Two million shirtless or ill-shirted workers sit enchanted in Workhouse Bastilles, five million more (according to some) in Ugolino Hunger-cellars; and for remedy you say,— what say you?—"Raise *our* rents!" I have not in my time heard any stranger speech, not even on the Shores of the Dead Sea. You continue addressing those poor shirt-spinners and over-producers in really a *too* triumphant manner!

"Will you bandy accusations, will you accuse *us* of over-production? We take the Heavens and the Earth to witness that we have produced nothing at all. Not from us proceeds this frightful overplus of shirts. In the wide domains of created Nature, circulates no shirt or thing of our producing. Certain fox-brushes nailed upon our stable-door, the fruit of fair audacity at Melton Mowbray; these we have produced, and they are openly nailed up there. He that accuses us of producing, let him shew himself, let him name what and when. We are innocent of producing;—ye ungrateful, what mountains of things have we not, on the contrary, had to "consume," and make away with! . . . Ye ungrateful!—and did you not grow under the shadow of our wings? Are not your filthy mills built on these fields of ours; on this soil of England, which belongs to—whom think you? And we shall not offer you our own wheat at the price that pleases us, but that partly pleases you? A precious notion! What would become of you, if we chose, at any time, to decide on growing no wheat more?"

CHAPTER XIII

DEMOCRACY

To what extent Democracy has now reached, how it advances irresistible with ominous, ever-increasing speed, he that will open his eyes on any province of human affairs may discern. Democracy is everywhere the inexorable demand of these ages, swift fulfilling itself. From the thunder of Napolean battles, to the jabbering of Open-vestry in St. Mary Axe, all things announce Democracy. . . .

But truly, as I have to remark in the meanwhile, "the liberty of not being oppressed by your fellow man" is an indispensable, yet one of the most insignificant fractional parts of Human Liberty. No man oppresses thee, can bid thee fetch or carry, come or go, without reason shown. True; from all men thou art emancipated: but from Thyself and from the Devil—? No man, wiser, unwiser, can make thee come or go: but thy own futilities, bewilderments, thy false appetites for Money, Windsor Georges and such like? . . . Thou art the thrall not of Cedric the Saxon, but of thy own brutal appetites. . . And thou pratest of thy "liberty?" Thou entire blockhead! . . .

Sure enough, of all paths a man could strike into, there *is,* at any given moment, a *best path* for every man; a thing which, here and now, it were of all things *wisest* for him to do;—which could he be but led to driven to do, he were then doing "like a man," as we phrase it; all men and gods agreeing with him, the whole Universe virtually exclaiming Well-done to him! His success, in such case, were complete; his felicity a maximum. This path, to find this path and walk in it, is the one thing needful for him. Whatsoever forwards him in that, let it come to him even in the shape of blows and spurnings, is liberty: whatsoever hinders him, were it wardmotes, open-vestries, poll-booths, tremendous cheers, rivers of heavy-wet, is slavery.

The notion that a man's liberty consists in giving his vote at election-hustings, and saying, "Behold, now I too have my twenty-thousandth part of a Talker in our National Palaver; will not all the gods be good to me?"—is one of the pleasantest! Nature nevertheless is kind at present; and puts it into the heads of many, almost of all. The liberty especially which has to purchase itself by social isolation, and each man standing separate from the other, having "no business with him" but a cash-account: this is such a liberty as the Earth seldom saw;—saw;— as the Earth will not long put up with, recommend it how you may.

Book IV
Horoscope
CHAPTER I
ARISTOCRACIES

. . . If the convulsive struggles of the last Half-Century have taught poor struggling convulsed Europe any truth, it may perhaps be this as the essence of innumerable others: That Europe requires a real Aristocracy, a real Priesthood, or it cannot continue to exist. Huge French Revolutions, Napoleonisms, then Bourbonisms with their corollary of Three Days, finishing in very unfinal Louis-Philippisms: all this ought to be didactic! All this may have taught us, That False Aristocracies are insupportable; that No-Aristocracies, Liberty-and-Equalities are impossible; that true Aristocracies are at once indispensable and not easily attained.

Aristocracy and Priesthood, a Governing Class and a Teaching Class: these two, sometimes separate and endeavoring to harmonise themselves, sometimes of conjoined as one, and the King a Pontiff-King:—there did no Society exist without these two vital elements, there will none exist. It lies in the very nature of man: you will visit no remotest village in the most republican country of the world, where virtually or actually you do not find these two powers at work. Man, little as he may suppose it, is necessitated to obey superiors. He is a social being in virtue of this necessity; nay he could not be gregarious otherwise. He obeys those whom he esteems better than himself, wiser, braver;

and will forever obey such and even be ready and delighted to do it. . . .

(Note: In the interest of clarity and logic, we have modified the order of Carlyle's chapters by placing here a selection from Book III.—The eds.)

CHAPTER XII

REWARD

All true work is sacred: in all true work, were it but hard labor there is something of divineness. . . .

Industrial work, still under bondage to Mammon, the rational soul of it not yet awakened, is a tragic spectacle . . . Yet courage: the beneficent Destines, kind in their sternness, are apprising us that this cannot continue. Labor is not a devil, even while encased in Mammonism; Labor is ever an imprisoned god, writhing unconsciously or consciously to escape out of Mammonism! Plugson of Undershop, like Taillefer of Normandy, wants victory; how much happier will even Plugson be to have a chivalrous victory than a Chactaw one! The unredeemed ugliness is that of a slothful People. Show me a People energetically busy; heaving, struggling, all shoulders at the wheel; their heart pulsing, every muscle swelling, with man's energy and will;—I show you a People of whom great good is already predictable; to whom all manner of good is yet certain, if their energy endure. By very working, they will learn; they have, Antaeus-like, their foot on Mother Fact: how can they but learn?

The vulgarest Plugson of a Master-Worker, who can command Workers, and get work out of them, is already a considerable man. Blessed and thrice-blessed symptoms I discern of Master-Workers who are not vulgar men; who are Nobles, and begin to feel that they must act as such: all speed to these, they are England's hope at present! But in this Plugson himself, conscious of almost no nobleness whatever, how much is there! Not without man's faculty, insight, courage, hard energy, is this rugged figure. His words none of the wisest; but his actings cannot be altogether foolish. Think, how were, stoodst thou suddenly in his shoes! He has to command a thousand men. And not imaginary commanding; no, it is real, incessantly practical. The evil passions of so many men (with the Devil in them, as in all of us) he has to vanquish; by manifold force of speech and of silence, to repress or evade. What a force of silence, to say nothing of the others, is in Plugson! For these his thousand men he has to provide raw-material, machinery, arrangement, houseroom; and ever at the week's end, wages by due sale. No Civil-List, or Goulburn-Baring Budget has he to fall back upon, for paying of his regiment; he has to pick his supplies from the confused face of the whole Earth and Contemporaneous History, by his dexterity alone. There will be dry eyes if he fails to do it!—He exclaims, at present, "black in the face," near strangled with Dilettante Legislation: "Let me have elbow-room, throat-room, and I will not fail! No I will spin yet, and conquer like a giant: what 'sinews of war', lie in me, untold resources toward the Conquest of this Planet, if instead of hanging me, you husband them, and help me!"—My indomitable friend, it is *true;* and thou shalt and must be helped.

CHAPTER IV
CAPTAINS OF INDUSTRY

If I believed that Mammonism with its adjuncts was to continue henceforth the one serious principle of our existence, I should reckon it idle to solicit remedial measures from any Government, the disease being insusceptible of remedy. Government can do much, but it can in no wise do all. Government, as the most conspicuous object in Society, is called upon to give signal of what shall be done; and, in many ways, to preside over, further, and command the doing of it. But the Government cannot do, by all its signaling and commanding, what the Society is radically indisposed to do. In the long-run every Government is the exact symbol of its People, with their wisdom and unwisdom; we have to say, Like People like Government.

The leaders of Industry, if Industry is ever to be led, are virtually the Captains of the World; if there be no nobleness in them, there will never be an Aristocracy more. . . . Let the Captains of Industry retire into their own hearts, and ask solemnly, If there is nothing but vulturous hunger, for fine wines, valet reputation and gilt carriages, discoverable there? Of hearts made by the Almighty God I will not believe such a thing. . . .

Awake ye noble Workers, warriors in the one true war: all

this must be remedied. It is you who are already half-alive, whom I will welcome into life, whom I will conjure in God's name to shake off your enchanted sleep, and live wholly! . . . Honour to you in your kind. It is to you I call: ye know at least this, That the mandate of God to His creature man is: Work! The future Epic of the World rests not with those that are near dead, but with those that are alive, and those that are coming into life.

CHAPTER VIII

THE DIDACTIC

But it is to you, ye Workers, who do already work, and are as grown men, noble and honourable in a sort, that the whole world calls for new work and nobleness. Subdue mutiny, discord, wide-spread despair, by manfulness, justice, mercy and wisdom. Chaos is dark, deep as Hell; let light be, and there is instead a green flowery World. Oh, it is great, and there is no other greatness. To make some nook of God's Creation a little fruitfuller, better, more worthy of God; to make some human hearts a little wiser, manfuler, happier,—more blessed, less accursed! It is a work for a God. Sooty Hell of mutiny and savagery and despair can, by man's energy, be made a kind of Heaven; cleared of its soot, of its mutiny, of its need to mutiny. . . .

Unstained by wasteful deformities, by wasted tears or heart's-blood of men, or any defacement of the Pit, noble fruitful Labour, growing ever nobler, will come forth,—the grand sole miracle of Man; whereby Man has risen from the low places of this Earth, very literally, into divine Heavens. Ploughers, Spinners, Builders; Prophets, Poets, Kings, Brindleys and Goethes, Odins and Arkwrights; all martyrs, and noble men, and gods are of one grand Host; immeasurable; Marching ever forward since the beginnings of the World. The enormous, all-conquering, flame-crowned Host, noble every soldier in it; sacred, and alone noble. Let him who is not of it hide himself. Stars at every button cannot make him noble; sheaves of Bathgarters, nor bushels of Georges; nor any other contrivance but manfully enlisting in it, valiantly taking place and step in it. O Heavens, will he not bethink himself; he too is so needed in the Host. It were so blessed, thrice-blessed, for himself and for us all! In hope of the last Partridge, and some Duke of Weimar among our English Dukes, we will be patient yet a while. . . .

CHARTISM (1837-1848)

The Chartist Movement was both a working class effort to obtain the ballot and what Marx and Engels regarded as the first genuine manifestation of the proletariat in action. In 1832 the British Parliament passed a reform bill giving representation to the industrial towns. The bill represented a major concession to the middle class, but the mass of the population continued to be excluded from political life. When the Parliament of 1837 refused further concessions, some of the Radicals joined the London Working Man's Association in drawing up a manifesto. "The People's Charter," demanded what came to be known as "the six points":

Universal Manhood Suffrage
Annual Parliaments
Payment of Members
Vote by Ballot
Equal Electoral Districts
Abolition of Property Qualifications for Members of Parliament

Organizations were formed and mass meetings held throughout the industrial regions of England. A year later the petition, with a million and a quarter signatures appended, was presented to Parliament. In 1848, the Year of Revolution, another petition, this time with six million signatures (many fictitious) was carried in procession to Parliament. Then the movement, discredited by riots and acts of violence, collapsed.

The *National Petition* (1839) given below was one of several drawn up by the leaders of the Chartist Movement.

NATIONAL PETITION (1839)

Unto the Honourable the Commons of the United Kingdom of Great Britain and Ireland in Parliament assembled, the Petition of the undersigned, their suffering countrymen.

Humbley Sheweth,

That we, your petitioners, dwell in a land whose merchants are noted for enterprise, whose manufacturers are very skilful, and whose workmen are proverbial for their industry. The land itself is goodly, the soil rich, and the temperature wholesome. It is abundantly furnished with the materials of commerce and trade. It has numerous and convenient harbours. In facility of internal communication it exceeds all others. For three and twenty years we have enjoyed a profound peace. Yet, with all these elements of national prosperity, and with every disposition and capacity to take advantage of them, we find ourselves overwhelmed with public and private suffering. We are bowed down under a load of taxes; which, notwithstanding, fall greatly short of the wants of our rulers. Our traders are trembling on the verge of bankruptcy; our workmen are starving. Capital brings no profit and labour no remuneration. The home of the artificer is desolate, and the warehouse of the pawnbroker is full. The workhouse is crowded, and the manufactory is deserted. We have looked on every side; we have searched diligently in order to find out the causes of a distress so sore and so long continued. We can discover none in nature, or in Providence. Heaven has dealt graciously by the people nor have the people abused its grace, but the foolishness of our rulers has made the goodness of God of none effect. The energies of a mighty kingdom have been wasted in building up the power of selfish and ignorant men, and its resources squandered for their aggrandisement. The good of a part has been advanced at the sacrifice of the good of the nation. The few have governed for the interest of the few, while the interests of the many have been sottishly neglected, or insolently and tyrannously trampled upon. It was the fond expectation of the friends of the people that a remedy for the greater part, if not for the whole, of their grievances, would be found in the Reform Act of 1832. They regarded that Act as a wise means to a worthy end, as the machinery of an improved legislation, when the will of the masses would be at length potential. They have been bitterly and basely deceived. The fruit which looked so fair to the eye has turned to dust and ashes when gathered. The Reform Act has effected a transfer of power from one domineering faction to another, and left the people as helpless as before. Our slavery has been exchanged for an apprenticeship to liberty, which has aggravated the painful feelings of our social degradation, by adding to it the sickening of still deferred hope. We come before your Honourable House to tell you, with all humility, that this state of things must not be permitted to continue. That it cannot long continue, without very seriously endangering the stability of the throne, and the peace of the kingdom, and that if, by God's help, and all lawful and constitutional appliances, an end can be put to it, we are fully resolved that it shall speedily come to an end. We tell your Honourable House, that the capital of the master must no longer be deprived of its due profit; that the labour of the workman must no longer be deprived of its due reward. That the laws which make food dear, and those which make money scarce must be abolished. That taxation must be made to fall on property, not on industry. That the good of the many, as it is the only legitimate end, so must it be the sole study of the Government. As a preliminary essential to these and other requisite changes—as the means by which alone the interests of the people can be effectually vindicated and secured, we demand that those interests be confided to the keeping of the people. When the State calls for defenders, when it calls for money, no consideration of poverty or ignorance can be pleaded in refusal or delay of the call. Required as we are, universally, to support and obey the laws, nature and reason entitle us to demand, that in the making of the laws, the universal voice shall be implicitly listened to. We perform the duties of freemen; we must have the privileges of freemen. We demand universal suffrage. The suffrage to be exempt from the corruption of the wealthy, and the violence of the powerful, must be secret. The assertion of our right necessarily involves the power of our uncontrolled exercise. We ask for the reality of a good, not for its semblance, therefore we demand the ballot. The connection between the representatives and the people, to be beneficial, must be intimate. The legislative and constituent powers, for correction and for instruction, ought to be brought into frequent contact. Errors which are comparatively light, when susceptible of a speedy popular remedy, may produce the most disastrous effects when permitted to grow inveterate through years of compulsory endurance. To public safety as well as public confidence, frequent elections are essential. Therefore, we demand annual Parliaments. With power to choose, and freedom in choosing, the range of our choice must be unrestricted. We are compelled by the existing laws, to take for our representatives, men who are incapable of appreciating our difficulties, or who have little sympathy with them; merchants who have retired from trade and no longer feel its harrassings; proprietors of land who are alike ignorant of its evils and their cure; lawyers by whom the notoriety of the senate is coveted only as a means of obtaining notice in the courts. The labours of a representative, who is sedulous in the discharge of his duty, are numerous and burdensome. It is neither just, nor reasonable, nor safe, that they should continue to be gratuitously rendered. We demand that in the future election of members of your Honourable House, the approbation of the constituency shall be the sole qualification, and that to every representative so chosen, shall be assigned, out of the public taxes, a fair and adequate remuneration for the time which he is called upon to devote to the public service. The management of this mighty kingdom has hitherto been a subject for contending factions to try their selfish experiments upon. We have felt the consequences in our sorrowful experience. Short glimmerings of uncertain enjoyment, swallowed up by long and dark seasons of suffering. If the self-government of the people should not remove their distresses, it will at least remove their repining. Universal suffrage will, and it alone can, bring true and lasting peace to the nation; we firmly believe that it will also bring prosperity. May it therefore please your Honourable House to take this petition intò your most serious consideration, and to use your utmost endeavours, by all constitutional means, to have a law passed, granting to every male of lawful age, sane mind, and unconvicted of crime, the right of voting for members of Parliament, and directing all future elections of members of Parliament to be in the way of secret ballot, and ordaining that the duration of Parliament, so chosen, shall in no case exceed one year, and abolishing all property qualifications in the members, and providing for their due remuneration while in attendance on their Parliamentary duties.

"And your petitioners shall ever pray."

SAINT-SIMON (1760-1825)

Claude-Henri de Rouvroy, Comte de Saint-Simon, was a descendant of one of the most illustrious noble houses of France, one that traced its ancestry back to Charlemagne. An army officer under the Old Regime government, he fought with distinction as a member of the French expeditionary force sent to support the American Revolution. When the French Revolution broke out, Saint-Simon abandoned his titles and joined the radical Jacobins, but he also acquired a new fortune speculating in the Revolutionary land sales. A lavish spender, he squandered his wealth entertaining the elite of French intellectual society, and the last years of his life, those in which he did his writing and in which he attracted a devoted band of disciples, were lived in abject poverty. The bulk of his writing appeared in fragmentary form, as articles for obscure journals or as pamphlets.

The selections that follow are from *Oeuvres choisies de Saint-Simon*, t. 3, Paris, 1859 (translations by the editors).

THE "PARABLE" OF SAINT-SIMON (1819)

Let us suppose that France suddenly lost her fifty leading physicists, chemists, physiologists, mathematicians, poets, painters, sculptors, musicians, writers; her fifty leading mechanical engineers, civil and military engineers, artillery experts, architects, doctors, surgeons, apothecaries, seamen, clockmakers; her fifty leading bankers, two hundred of her leading merchants, six hundred of her leading cultivators of the soil, fifty of her leading ironmasters, arms manufacturers, tanners, dyers, miners, clothmakers, cotton manufacturers, silk-makers, linen-makers, manufacturers of hardware, of crystal and glassware, of faience and porcelain, ship builders, carriers, printers, engravers, goldsmiths and other fine metal workers; fifty of her leading masons, carpenters, joiners, farriers, locksmiths, cutlers, die-casters, and the hundred others of unspecified occupations, the most competent in the sciences, fine arts and crafts, making in all the three thousand leading savants, artists and productive personnel of France.

Since these are the essential French producers, those who are responsible for the most important products, those who direct the works most useful to the nation and who render the sciences, the fine arts and the crafts fruitful, they are really the flower of French society, they are of all Frenchmen the most useful to their country, those who procure the most glory, who add most to its civilization as well as its prosperity: the nation would become a body without a soul at the instant it lost them; it would fall immediately into a state of inferiority in relation to the nations that today are its rivals, and it would continue to remain subordinate so long as it failed to repair this loss, so long as it failed to grow another head. It would take France an entire generation to repair such a misfortune because the men who distinguish themselves in works of positive utility are rare exceptions, and nature is not prodigal of exceptions, above all of this kind.

Let us pass to another assumption. Let us suppose that France keeps all the men of genius it possesses in the sciences, the fine arts and the crafts, but that it has the misfortune to lose, on the same day, Monsieur, the king's brother, Monseigneur le duc d'Angouleme, Monseigneur le duc de Berry, Monseigneur le duc d'Orleans, Monseigneur le duc de Bourbon, Madame la duchesse d'Angouleme, Madame la duchesse de Berry, Madame la duchesse d'Orleans, Madame la duchesse de Bourbon, and Mademoiselle de Conde.

Let us suppose that she loses at the same time all the high officers of the royal household, all the ministers of state, with or without portfolio, all the councilors of state, all the chief magistrates, all the marshals, cardinals, archbishops, bishops, grand vicars and canons, all the prefects and sub-prefects, all the officials in the ministries, all the judges, and besides that, ten thousand of the wealthiest landowners who live nobly.

This accident would certainly distress the French people because they are kind-hearted, because they could not view with indifference the sudden disappearance of such a large number of their compatriots. But this loss of thirty thousand of the reputedly most important individuals in the state would evoke sorrow solely on sentimental grounds, for no political harm would result for the state.

First because it would be easy to fill the places that would become vacant; there exist an ample number of Frenchmen capable of exercising the functions of brother to the king as well as Monsieur; many are capable of filling the roles of princes as well as Monseigneur le duc d'Angouleme, Monsieur le duc d'Orleans, Monsieur le duc de Bourbon; many Frenchwomen would make as good princesses as Madame la duchesse d'Angouleme, Madame la duchesse de Berry or Mesdames d'Orleans, de Bourbon and de Conde.

The ante-chambers of the chateau are full of courtiers ready to take the places of the high officers of the royal household; the army possesses ample numbers of soldiers as fit to direct troops as our present marshals. How many heads of departments are the equal of our ministers of state! How many administrators would better handle the districts than the prefects and sub-prefects now in office! How many lawyers would make as good legal counselors as our present judges! How many priests would serve as capably as our cardinals, archbishops, grand vicars and canons! As for the ten thousand proprietors living nobly, their heirs would need no apprenticeship to do the honors of their salons as well as they.

The prosperity of France can result only from the progress of science, the fine arts and the crafts; now the princes, the high dignitaries of the royal household, the bishops, the marshals, the prefects, and the idle landowners do not contribute directly to the progress of science, the fine arts and the crafts; far from contributing to them, they can only hinder them since they insist on prolonging the preponderance conjecture has thus far exercised over positive knowledge! They necessarily stand in the way of the prosperity of the nation by, so far as they can, depriving the savants, the productive persons, of that primacy that is their legitimate due. They stand in the way of it by utilizing their wealth in a manner that is useless to the sciences, arts and crafts; they hinder it because annually they take from the taxes paid by the nation a sum of three to four hundred millions under the guise of salaries, pensions, gratifications, indemnities, etc., all to pay for labors that are useless.

These suppositions suggest the most important fact of present day politics; they provide a perspective from which one gains, at a glance, an insight into the situation in all its enormity. They prove clearly, though indirectly, that the social order is far from being perfected; that men are still letting themselves be exploited by violence and sham; and that the human race (politically speaking) is still plunged in immorality:

For the savants, artists and producers whose work, alone, is of positive utility to society, and who cost it almost nothing, are held in subordinate roles by princes and others of the governing class who are only more-or-less incompetent time servers;

For those who are charged with administering public affairs

every year share among themselves half the revenues and yet fail to use a third of the taxes, out of what they personally fail to pocket, in a manner that would be beneficial to the citizenry.

These suppositions permit one to recognize that society, as constituted, is truly a world turned upside down:

For the nation has accepted as a fundamental principle the rule that the poor should be generous to the rich, and that, consequently, those worst off should be deprived each day of a part of their necessities in order to augment the superfluity of the great proprietors;

For the most culpable, the wholesale thieves, those who oppress the mass of the citizenry and who every year extract three or four hundred millions, find themselves entrusted with the task of punishing the petty infractions of the rules of society;

For ignorance, sloth and a taste for expensive pleasures form the appanage of the leaders of society, and the men who are capable, economical and hard working are employed solely as subordinates and instruments;

For, in a word, in all kinds of occupations, the incompetent people are charged with directing the competent; with regard to morality, the most immoral are expected to train citizens in virtue; and with regard to administrative justice, the big crooks are chosen to punish the faults of the petty delinquents.

Although this extract may be short, we believe we have sufficiently proved that the body politic is sick; that its malady is serious and dangerous; that it is as critical as it could be for the whole and all its parts are affected at one and the same time.

EXTRACT FROM THE "ORGANIZER" (1820)

We believe we can take it for granted that, in the new political order, the social organization should have for its sole and permanent object the best possible application to the needs of men of that knowledge acquired through the sciences, the fine arts and the crafts; of expanding that knowledge, of perfecting it, and of increasing it so far as possible. . . .

This is not the place to represent in detail the astonishing degree of prosperity society might attain with such an organization; it is easy enough to imagine; and we shall limit ourselves to hinting at it through the following observations:

Up to the present, the efforts men applied to nature

were purely individual and isolated. Furthermore, their energies always have been in large part wasted, for mankind up to now has been divided into two unequal fractions, of which the smaller has constantly employed all its energies, and often even a portion of those of the greater, to dominating the latter; while the latter has consumed a considerable part of its abilities in repulsing that domination. It is certain, none the less, that, despite this enormous loss of energy, mankind has achieved, in the most civilized countries, a remarkable degree of ease and prosperity. One may judge from that to what point it might have obtained if there had been almost no waste effort, if men, ceasing to order one another about, had organized to apply their combined efforts to nature, and if the nations pursued together the same system.

THE INDUSTRIAL SYSTEM: PART ONE (1821)

Address to Philanthropists

Gentlemen. — The passion that animates you is of divine institution; it places you in the front rank among christians, it gives you the rights, it imposes on you the duty to combat evil passions and to struggle shoulder to shoulder with the people and with kings when they allow themselves to be led by the people.

Your predecessors have begun the social organization of humanity, it is for you to terminate this holy enterprise. The first christians have founded morality by preaching in the thatched cottages, as in the palaces, the divine principle: *All men must regard each other as brothers, they must love and aid one another.* They dreamed of a doctrine in accord with this principle, but that doctrine received from them only a philosophical character; and to you is reserved the honor of organizing the temporal power in conformity with this divine axiom. . . .

First question.—What are the principal political changes that will be operative during the fourth epoch of christianity?

Response.—I believe that during this fourth epoch a new spiritual and a new temporal power will be organized.

I believe that the new spiritual power will be composed originally of all the existing Academies of Science existing in Europe, and of all the persons who merit being admitted into these scientific corporations. I believe that once this nucleus is formed, those who compose it will organize themselves. I believe that the direction of education, including public education, will be entrusted to this new spiritual power. I believe that the pure morality of the Gospel will serve as the base for the new public instruction, and that for most it will be pushed as far as possible in accord with positive knowledge, proportionate to the time that children of differing levels of wealth can spend in the schools. . . .

I believe that in each European nation the administration of temporal affairs will be entrusted to the entrepreneurs of peaceful works who will employ the largest numbers of individuals, and I am persuaded that this administration, as a direct result of the personal interest of the administrators, will occupy itself first of all with maintaining peace among the nations, and finally with diminishing, so far as possible, the tax burden, as well as in employing the proceeds in a manner most advantageous to the community.

Here are the three reasons on which I found this opinion:

1. These new bases of social organization, being in strict conformity to the interests of the immense majority of the population, ought to be regarded as a general political truth deduced from the principle of divine morality:

All men should regard each other as brothers; they should love and aid one another.

Thus God evidently intended that in the present state of enlightenment, christian society should be constituted in this manner.

2. Humanly speaking, and without raising ourselves above the level of scientific facts, this constitution of christian society is the natural consequence and the immediate effect of the destruction of slavery, as well as of the superiority acquired by the sciences based on observation over theology and the other branches of metaphysics.

3. By limiting ourselves to political considerations, it is evident that the progress of civilization will lead to this result; because the positive forces, as much intellectual as material, today find themselves in the hands of those who profess the sciences based on observation and of those who undertake and direct the industrial enterprises. It is only because of the effect of age-old habit that society bears the yoke of nobles and theologians. Now, experience has proven that society always disencumbers itself of habits contracted in the past when those habits are found contrary to its interests, and that it discovers new

means of satisfying it needs; it is then indubitable that it will abandon the institutions of the clergy and nobility; it is also indubitable that political power will pass into the hands of those who already possess almost all the social forces, of those who daily direct the physical forces, of those who create the pecuniary forces, of those, finally, who continually augment the intellectual forces.

Second question.—What force will determine these changes, and by whom will this force be directed?

Response.—The force of moral sentiment will determine these changes, and this force will have for its principal impulsion the belief that all political principles ought to be deduced from the general principle that God has given to men.

Those who will direct this force will be the philanthropists; They will be on this occasion, just as in the foundation of christianity, the direct agents of the *Eternal*.

By their first common effort the philanthropists have brought acceptance of the principle of divine morality to the powers of the earth; by a second general effort, philanthropy will lead nobles and theologians to support the general consequences of this principle. . . .

I have worked for six years and with much ardor to demonstrate to savants and industrialists:

1. That at this moment society manifests an evident tendency to organize itself in a manner most favorable to the progress of the sciences and the prosperity of industry.

2. That to organize society in a manner most favorable to the progress of the sciences and the prosperity of industry it is necessary to entrust the spiritual power to savants, and the administration of temporal power to the industrialists.

3. That the savants and industrialists can organize society in a manner conforming to its desires and needs, since the savants possess the intellectual forces and the industrialists dispose of the material forces. . . .

Third question.—What means will the philanthropists employ to reorganize society?

Response.—The sole means the philanthropists will employ will be that of exposition, partly verbal, partly by writing. They will preach to kings that it is their duty as christians, and to their interest for the preservation of their hereditary powers, to confide the direction of public education, as well as the labor of perfecting doctrines, to the savants, and the responsibility of directing temporal affairs to the industrialists who are most competent in administrative matters.

They will preach to the people that they ought unanimously to manifest to princes the desire that the conduct of temporal and spiritual affairs be entirely abandoned to the class most capable of directing them in the sense of the general interest, and to those most interested in giving them this direction.

The philanthropists will continue their verbal and written exposition throughout the time required to induce princes (by the effect of conviction or by that of the all-powerful influence of public opinion), to effect the changes in the social organization that the progress of enlightenment, the common interest of all the population, and the imminent and immediate interest of the very great majority demands.

In a word, the sole means that will be employed by the philanthropists will be that of exposition; and the sole object that they will propose in their expositions will be that of inducing kings to use their powers to bring about the political changes that have become necessary. . . .

Gentlemen, some of those who have been most marked in the ranks of the ultras, the Jacobins, or the Bonapartists, are perhaps those God has chosen by preference to become founders of the new christianity, of the definitive christianity, of the one that will be entirely disengaged from the superstitions with which the ambitious views of the clergy have overburdened them, and who have been affected by the ignorance of our fathers. In a word, let us take in the heretics in morality and politics, provided that they frankly abjure their heresies and that they work with zeal for the establishment of the true doctrine.

Prudent and moderate men are quite satisfactory for maintaining an established order of things, they are even capable of introducing slight modifications; but they lack the energy necessary to effect great ameliorations. The first christians were passionate men, the new ones must be so likewise, and passionate men, by the nature of their character, are exposed to commiting great errors. The apostle Paul began as one of the most ardent enemies of christianity.   I have the honor of being, Gentlemen,

Your very obedient servant,

Henri Saint-Simon

ROBERT OWEN (1771-1858)

The son of a Welsh shopkeeper, Robert Owen was a shining example of the nineteenth century self-made business-man, but one who earned the bitter hatred of his class. He left school at the age of nine to become an apprentice. By his early twenties he was a substantial manufacturer of cloth, and at twenty-eight, with a group of associates, he pur-chased the New Lanark mills in Scotland. There he gained an international reputation both for the efficiency of his fac-tory and for the model village created to house his workers. His concern for the education and well-being of children led him to urge a law drastically curtailing child labor; the economic distress that followed the Napoleonic Wars turned him toward more sweeping social changes. Disappointed by the reception accorded his *Report to the County of Lanark,* in which he argued the advantages of a socialist community, he attempted to found such a community at New Harmony in America. When that failed, he organized a large, if short-lived, trade union in Great Britain and devoted the last years of his life to experiments with cooperatives and free labor exchanges.

The selection below is from his celebrated *Report to the County of Lanark* (Glasgow, 1821), the subtitle of which reads "of a Plan for Relieving Public Distress, and Removing Discontent, by Giving Permanent, Productive Employment, to the Poor and Working Classes; Under Arrangements which will Essentially Improve their Character, and Ameliorate their Condition; Diminish the Expenses of Pro-duction and Consumption, and Create Markets Co-extensive with Production."

REPORT TO THE COUNTY OF LANARK (1821)

PART I—INTRODUCTION

The evil for which your Reporter has been required to provide a remedy, is the general want of employment, at wages sufficient to support the family of a working man beneficially for the community. After the most earnest consideration of the subject, he has been compelled to conclude, that such em-ployment cannot be procured through the medium of trade, commerce, or manufactures, or even of agriculture, until the Gov-ernment and the Legislature, cordially supported by the country, shall previously adopt measures to remove obstacles, which, without their interference, will now permanently keep the working classes in poverty and discontent, and gradually deteriorate all the resources of the empire.

Your Reporter has been impressed with the truth of this conclusion by the following considerations:

First.—That manual labour, properly directed, is the source of all wealth, and of national prosperity.

Second.—That, when properly directed, labour is of far more value to the community than the expense necessary to maintain the labourer in considerable comfort.

Third.—That manual labour, properly directed, may be made to continue of this value in all parts of the world, under any supposable increase of its population, for many centuries to come.

Fourth.—That, under a proper direction of manual labour, Great Britain and its dependencies may be made to support an incalculable increase of population, most advantageously for all its inhabitants.

Fifth.—That when manual labour shall be so directed, it will be found that population cannot, for many years, be stimulated to advance as rapidly as society might be benefited by its increase.

These considerations, deduced from the first and most obvious principles of the science of political economy, convinced your Reporter that some formidable artificial obstacle intervened to obstruct the natural improvement and progress of society.

It is well known that, during the last half-century in particular, Great Britain, beyond any other nation, has progressively increased its powers of production, by a rapid advancement in scientific improvements and arrangements, introduced, more or less, into all the departments of productive industry throughout the empire.

The amount of this new productive power cannot, for want of proper data, be very accurately estimated; but your Reporter has ascertained, from facts which none will dispute, that its increase has been enormous;—that, compared with the manual labour of the whole population of Great Britain and Ireland, it is, at least, as 40 to 1, and may be easily as 100 to 1; and that this increase may be extended to other countries; that it is already sufficient to saturate the world with wealth, and that the power of creating wealth may be made to advance perpetually in an accelerating ratio. It appeared to your Reporter that the natural effect of the aid thus obtained from knowledge and science should be to add to the wealth and happiness of society in proportion as the new power increased and was judiciously directed; and that, in consequence, all parties would thereby be substantially benefited. All know, however, that these beneficial effects do not exist. On the contrary, it must be acknowledged that the working classes, which form so large a proportion of the population, cannot obtain even the comforts which their labour formerly procured for them, and that no party appears to gain, but all to suffer, by their distress.

Having taken this view of the subject, your Reporter was induced to conclude that the want of beneficial employment for the working classes, and the consequent public distress, were owing to the rapid increase of the new productive power, for the advantageous application of which, society had neglected to make the proper arrangements. Could these arrangements be formed, he entertained the most confident expectation that productive employment might again be found for all who required it; and that the national distress, of which all now so loudly complain, might be gradually converted into a much higher degree of prosperity than was attainable prior to the extraordinary accession lately made to the productive powers of society.

Cheered by such a prospect, your Reporter directed his attention to the consideration of the possibility of devising arrangements by means of which the whole population might participate in the benefits derivable from the increase of scientific productive power; and he has the satisfaction to state to the meeting, that he has strong grounds to believe that such arrangements are practicable. . . .

PART II—OUTLINES OF THE PLAN

It is admitted that under the present system no more hands can be employed advantageously in agriculture or manufactures; and that both interests are on the eve of bankruptcy. It is also admitted that the prosperity of the country, or rather that which ought to create prosperity, the improvement in mechanical and chemical science, has enabled the population to produce more than the present system permits to be consumed. In consequence, new arrangements become necessary, by which *consumption* may be made to keep pace with *production,* and the following are recommended:

First.—To cultivate the soil with the spade instead of the plough.

Second.—To make such changes as the spade cultivation requires, to render it easy and profitable to individuals, and beneficial to the country.

Third.—To adopt a standard of value by means of which the exchange of the products of labour may proceed without check or limit, until wealth shall become so abundant that any further increase to it will be considered useless, and will not be desired.

We proceed to give the reasons for recommending these arrangements in preference to all others. And first, those for preferring the spade to the plough for the universal cultivation of the soil.

Practical cultivators of the soil know, that the most favourable circumstance for promoting the growth of vegetation is a due supply of moisture, and that when this is provided for, a good general crop seldom, if ever, fails. Water enters so largely into the food of all plants that if its *gradual* supply can be secured, the farmer and horticulturist feel assured of a fair return for their labour. Whatever mode of cultivation, therefore, can best effect the object of drawing off from the seed or plant an excess of water, and retaining this surplus as a reservoir from which a gradual supply of moisture may be obtained as required, must possess decided advantages.

It is also known to all practical agriculturists, that to obtain the best crops, the soil ought to be well broken and separated; and that the nearer it is brought to a garden mould, the more perfect is the cultivation. . . .

These facts being incontrovertible, few perhaps will hesitate to admit them. But it may be said that, admitting the statement to be true to the full extent, yet the plough, with a pair of horses and one man, performs so much work in a given time that, with all its imperfections, it may be a more economical instrument for the purpose required. Such has been the almost universal impression for ages past, and, in consequence, the plough has superseded the spade, and is considered to be an improved machine for ordinary cultivation.

All this is plausible, and is sanctioned by the old prejudices of the world; but your Reporter maintains that it is not true that the plough is, or has ever been, in any stage of society, the most economical instrument for the cultivation of the soil. It has been so in appearance only, not in reality.

Cultivated as the soil has been hitherto, the direct expense of preparing it by the plough (in the manner in which the plough prepares it) has been in many cases less per acre than it would have been by the spade. The increased crop which the latter implement would have produced, all other circumstances being the same, does not seem to have been taken into account, or to have been accurately ascertained, except by Mr. Falla, of Gateshead, near Newcastle, who, for many years, has had a hundred acres under spade cultivation, chiefly for nursery purposes, and who, by his practical knowledge of the subject, has realized, as your Reporter is informed, a large fortune. He has satisfactorily proved, by the experiments of four successive years, that although the expense of cultivation by the spade exceeds that of the plough per acre, yet the increased value of the crop greatly overbalances the increased expense of cultivation, and that even with "things as they are" the spade is a much better, and also a much more economical instrument with which to cultivate the soil, than the plough. . . .

Hitherto, those who have cultivated the soil for profit have generally been men trained to be tenacious of old-established practices, all their ideas have been confined within a very narrow range; they have not been taught to think about anything, till lately, except that which was in the common routine of their daily practice. . . . They must acquire as accurate a knowledge of *human* nature as they now possess of common *animal* nature.

Agriculture, instead of being, as heretofore, the occupation of the mere peasant and farmer, with minds as defective in their cultivation as their soils, will then become the delightful employment of a race of men, trained in the best habits and dispositions; familiar with the most useful practice in the arts and sciences; and with minds fraught with the most valuable information, and extensive general knowledge,—capable of forming and conducting combined arrangements in agriculture, trade, commerce, and manufactures, far superior to those which have yet existed in any of these departments, as they have been hitherto disjoined, and separately conducted. It will be readily perceived, that this is an advance in civilization and general improvement, that is to be effected solely *through the science of the influence of circumstances over human nature, and the knowledge of the means by which those circumstances may be easily controlled.*

Closet theorists, and inexperienced persons, suppose, that to exchange the plough for the spade, would be to turn back in the road of improvement,—to give up a superior for an inferior implement of cultivation. Little do they imagine, that the introduction of the spade, with the scientific arrangements which it requires, will produce far greater improvements in agriculture, than the steam engine has effected in manufactures. . . .

The introduction of the steam engine, and the spinning machine, added, in an extraordinary manner, to the powers of human nature. In their consequences they have, in half a century, multiplied the productive power, or the means of creating wealth, among the population of these islands, more than 12 fold, besides giving a great increase to the means of creating wealth in other countries.

The steam engine and spinning machines, with the endless mechanical inventions to which they have given rise, have, however, inflicted evils on society, which now greatly overbalance the benefits which are derived from them. They have created an aggregate of wealth, and placed it in the hands of a few, who, by its aid, continue to absorb the wealth produced by the industry of the many. Thus the mass of the population are become mere slaves to the ignorance and caprice of these monopolists, and are far more truly helpless and wretched than they were before the names of WATT and ARKWRIGHT were known. Yet these celebrated and ingenious men have been the instruments of preparing society for the important beneficial changes which are about to occur.

All now know and feel, that the good which these inventions are calculated to impart to the community, has not yet been realized. The condition of society, instead of being improved, has been deteriorated, under the new circumstances to which they have given birth; and is now experiencing a retrograde movement.

"Something," therefore, "must be done," as the general voice exclaims, to give to our suffering population, and to society at large, the means of deriving from these inventions the advantages which all men of science expect from them.

. . . The arrangements to which your Reporter now calls the

attention of the Public, present the certain means of renovating the moral character, and of improving, to an unlimited extent, the general condition of the population, and while they lead to a far more rapid multiplication of wealth than the present system permits to take place, they will effectually preclude all the evils with which wealth is now accompanied.

It is estimated, that, in Great Britain and Ireland, there are now under cultivation upwards of 60 millions of acres; and of these, 20 millions are arable, and 40 millions in pasture;—that, under the present system of cultivation by the plough, and of pasturing, about 2 millions at most of *actual labourers* are employed on the soil, giving immediate support to about three times that number, and supplying food for a population of about 18 millions. Sixty millions of acres, under a judicious arrangement of spade cultivation, with manufactures as an appendage, might be made to give healthy advantageous employment to 60 millions of labourers at the least, and support, in high comfort, a population greatly exceeding 100 millions. But, in the present low state of population in these islands, not more than 5 or 6 millions of acres could be properly cultivated by the spade, although all the operative manufacturers were to be chiefly in this mode of agriculture. Imperfect, therefore, as the plough is for the cultivation of the soil, it is probable, that, in this country, for want of an adequate population, many centuries will elapse before it can be entirely superseded by the spade; yet, under the plough system, Great Britain and Ireland are even now supposed to be greatly overpeopled.

It follows from this statement, that we possess the means of supplying the labouring poor, however numerous they may be, with permanent beneficial employment for many centuries to come. . . .

These incalculably increased products will render gold, the old artificial standard of value, far more unfit for the task which is to be performed than it was in 1797, when it ceased to be the British legal standard of value, or than it is now, when wealth has so much increased.

Your Reporter is of opinion, that the natural standard of human labour, fixed to represent its natural worth, or power of creating new wealth, will alone be found adequate to the purposes required.

To a mind coming first to this subject, innumerable and apparently insurmountable difficulties will occur; but by the steady application of that fixed and persevering attention, which is alone calculated successfully to contend against and overcome difficulties, every obstacle will vanish, and the practice will prove simple and easy.

That which can create new wealth, is of course worth the wealth which it creates. Human labour, whenever common justice shall be done to human beings, can now be applied to produce, advantageously for all ranks in society, many times the amount of wealth that is necessary to support the individual in considerable comfort. Of this new wealth so created, the labourer who produces it is justly entitled to his fair proportion; and the best interests of every community require that the producer should have a fair and fixed proportion of all the wealth which he creates. This can be assigned to him on no other principle, than by forming arrangements by which the *natural* standard of value shall become the *practical* standard of value. To make labour the standard of value, it is necessary to ascertain the amount of it in all articles to be bought and sold. This is, in fact, already accomplished, and is denoted, by what in commerce is technically termed, "the prime cost," or the net value of the whole labour contained in any article of value,—the material contained in, or consumed by, the manufacture of the article, forming a part of the whole labour.

The great object of society is, to obtain wealth, and to enjoy it.

The genuine principle of barter was, to exchange the supposed prime cost of, or value of labour, in one article, against the prime cost of, or amount of labour contained in any other article. This is the only equitable principle of exchange; but, as inventions increased, and human desires multiplied, it was found to be inconvenient in practice. Barter was succeeded by commerce, the principle of which is, to produce or procure every article at the lowest, and to obtain for it in exchange, the *highest* amount of labour. To effect this, an artificial standard of value was necessary; and the metals were, by common consent among nations, permitted to perform the office. This principle, in the progress of its operation, has been productive of important advantages, and of very great evils; but, like barter, it has been suited to a certain stage of society. It has stimulated invention; it has given industry and talent to the human character, and secured the future exertion of those energies which otherwise might have remained dormant and unknown. But it has made man ignorantly, individually selfish; placed him in opposition to his fellows; engendered fraud and deceit; blindly urged him forward to create, but deprived him of the wisdom to enjoy. In striving to take advantage of others, he has overreached himself. The strong hand of necessity will now force him into the path which conducts to that wisdom in which he has been so long deficient. He will discover the advantages to be derived from uniting in practice the best parts of the principles of barter and commerce and dismissing those which experience has proved to be inconvenient and injurious. This substantial improvement in the progress of society, may be easily effected by exchanging all articles with each other at their prime cost, or with reference to the amount of labour in each, which can be equitably ascertained, and by permitting the exchange to be made through a convenient medium to represent this value, and which will thus represent a real and unchanging value, and be issued only as substantial wealth increases. The profit of production will arise, in all cases, from the value of the labour contained in the article produced, and it will be for the interest of society that this profit should be most ample. Its exact amount will depend upon what, by strict examination, shall be proved to be the present real value of a day's labour; calculated with reference to the amount of wealth, in the necessaries and comforts of life, which an average labourer may, by temperate exertions, be now made to produce. . . .

PART III—DETAILS OF THE PLAN

This part of the Report naturally divides itself under the following heads, each of which shall be considered separately, and the whole, afterwards, in connexion, as forming an improved practical system for the working classes, highly beneficial, in whatever light it may be viewed, to every part of society:

First.—The number of persons who can be associated to give the greatest advantages to themselves and to the community.

Second.—The extent of the land to be cultivated by such association.

Third.—The arrangements for feeding, lodging, and clothing the population, and for training and educating the children.

Fourth.—Those for forming and superintending the establishments.

Fifth.—The disposal of the surplus produce, and the relation which will subsist between the several establishments.

Sixth.—Their connexion with the Government of the country and with general society.

The first object, then, of the political economist, in forming these arrangements, must be, to consider well under what limitation of numbers, individuals should be associated to form the first nucleus or division of society. All his future proceedings will be materially influenced by the decision of this point, which is one of the most difficult problems in the science of political economy. It will affect essentially the future character of individuals, and influence the general proceedings of mankind. It is, in fact, the corner-stone of the whole fabric of human society. The consequences, immediate and remote, which depend upon it, are so numerous and important, that to do justice to this part of the arrangement alone would require a work of many volumes. To form anything resembling a rational opinion on this subject, the mind must steadily survey the various effects which have arisen from associations which accident has hitherto combined in the history of the human species; and it should have a distinct idea of the results which other associations are capable of producing. Thus impressed with the magnitude and importance of the subject, after many years of deep and anxious reflection, and viewing it with reference to an improved spade cultivation, and to all the purposes of society, your Reporter ventures to recommend the formation of such arrangements as will unite about 300 men, women, and children, in their natural proportions, as the *minimum,* and about 2,000 as the *maximum,* for the future associations of the cultivators of the soil, who will be employed also in such additional occupations as may be advantageously annexed to it. In coming to this conclusion your Reporter never lost sight of that only sure guide to the political economist, the principle, *that it is the interest of all men, whatever may be their present artificial station in society, that there should be the largest amount of intrinsically valuable produce created, at the least expense of labour, and in a way the most advantageous to the producers and society.* . . Recommending, then, from 300 to 2,000, according to the localities of the farm or village, as the number of persons who should compose the associations for the new system of spade husbandry, we now proceed to consider—

Second,—The extent of land to be cultivated by such association.

This will depend upon the quality of the soil and other local considerations. Great Britain and Ireland, however, do not possess a population nearly sufficient to culivate our *best* soils in the most advantageous manner. It would therefore be nationally impolitic to place these associations upon *inferior* lands, which, in consequence, may be dismissed from present consideration. . . . Improved arrangements for the working classes will, in almost all cases, place the workman in the midst of his food, which it will be as beneficial for him to create as to consume. Sufficient land, therefore, will be allotted to these cultivators, to enable them to raise an abundant supply of food and the necessaries of life for themselves, and as much additional agricultural produce as the public demands may require from such a portion of the population. Under a well-devised arrangement for the working classes they will all procure for themselves the necessaries and comforts of life in so short a time, and so easily and pleasantly, that the occupation will be experienced to be little more than a recreation, sufficient to keep them in the best health and spirits for rational enjoyment of life. The surplus produce from the soil will be required only for the higher classes, those who live without manual labour, and those whose nice manual operations will not permit them at any time to be employed in agriculture and gardening. Of the latter, very few, if any, will be necessary, as mechanism may be made to supersede such operations, which are almost always injurious to health.

Under this view of the subject, the quantity of land which it would be the most beneficial for these associations to cultivate, with reference to their own well-being and the interests of society, will probably be from half an acre to an acre and a half for each individual. An association, therefore, of twelve hundred persons would require from 600 to 1800 statute acres, according as it may be intended to be more or less agricultural . . .

Third,—The arrangement for feeding, lodging, and clothing the population, and for training and educating the children. . . .

As it will afterwards appear that the food for the whole population can be provided better and cheaper under one general arrangement of cooking, and that the children can be better trained and educated together under the eye of their parents than under any other circumstances, a large square, or rather parallelogram, will be found to combine the greatest advantages in its form for the domestic arrangements of the association. This form, indeed, affords so many advantages for the comfort of human life, that if great ignorance respecting the means necessary to secure good conduct and happiness among the working classes had not prevailed in all ranks, it must long ago have become universal. It admits of a most simple, easy, convenient, and economical arrangement for all the purposes required. The four sides of this figure may be adapted to contain all the private apartments or sleeping and sitting rooms for the adult part of the population; general sleeping apartments for the children while under tuition; store-rooms, or warehouses in which to deposit various products; an inn, or house for the accommodation of strangers; an infirmary; &c., &c. In a line across the center of the parallelogram, leaving free space for air and light, and easy communication, might be erected the church, or places for worship; the schools; kitchen and apartments for eating; all in the most convenient situation for the whole population, and under the best possible public superintendence, without trouble, expense or inconvenience to any party. . . .

It has been, and still is, a received opinion among theorists in political economy, that man can provide better for himself, and more advantageously for the public, when left to his own individual exertions, opposed to, and in competition with his fellows, than when aided by any social arrangements, which shall unite his interests individually and generally with society. This principle of individual interest, opposed, as it is perpetually, to the public good is considered, by the most celebrated political economists, to be the corner stone of the social system, and without which, society could not subsist. Yet when they shall know themselves, and discover the wonderful effects, which combination and unity can produce, they will acknowledge that the present arrangement of society is the most antisocial, impolitic, and irrational, that can be devised; that under its influence, all the superior and valuable qualities of human nature are repressed from infancy, and that the most unnatural means are used to bring out the most injurious propensities; in short, that the utmost pains are taken to make that which by nature is the most delightful compound for producing excellence and happiness, absurd, imbecile, and wretched. Such is the conduct now pursued by those who are called the best and wisest of the present generation, although there is not one rational object to be gained by it. From this principle of individual interest have arisen all the divisions of mankind, the endless errors and mischiefs of class, sect, party, and of national antipathies, creating the angry and malevolent passions, and all the crimes and misery with which the human race has been hitherto afflicted. In short, if there be one closet doctrine more contrary to truth than another, it is the notion that individual interest, as the term is now understood, is a more advantageous principle on which to found the social system, for the benefit of all, or of any, than the principle of union and mutual cooperation. The former acts like an immense weight to repress the most valuable faculties and dispositions, and to give a wrong direction to all the human powers. It is one of those magnificent errors (if the expression may be allowed) that when enforced in practice, brings ten thousand evils in its train. The principle on which these economists proceed, instead of adding to the wealth of nations or of individuals, is itself the sole cause of poverty; and but for its operation, wealth would long ago have ceased to be a subject of contention in any part of the world. If, it may be asked, experience has proved that union, combination, and extensive arrangement among mankind, are a thousand times more powerful to *destroy,* than the efforts of an unconnected multitude, where each acts individually for himself,— would not a similar increased effect be produced by union, combination, and extensive arrangement, to *create and conserve?* Why should not the result be the same in the one case as in the other? But it is well known that a combination of men and of interests, can effect that which it would be futile to attempt, and impossible to accomplish, by individual exertions and separate interests. Then why, it may be inquired, have men so long acted individually, and in opposition to each other?

This is an important question, and merits the most serious attention.

Men have not yet been trained in principles that will permit them *to act in unison,* except to defend themselves or to destroy others. For self-preservation, they were early compelled to unite for these purposes in war. A necessity, however, equally powerful will now compel men to be trained to act together, to *create and conserve,* that in like manner they may preserve life in peace. Fortunately for mankind, the system of individal opposing interests, has now reached the extreme point of error and inconsistency;—in the midst of the most ample means to create wealth, all are in poverty, or in imminent danger, from the effects of poverty upon others.

The reflecting part of mankind, have admitted in theory, that the characters of men are formed chiefly by the circumstances in which they are placed; yet the science of the influence of circumstances, which is the most important of all the sciences, remains unknown for the great practical business of life. When it shall be fully developed, it will be discovered, that to unite the mental faculties of men, for the attainment of pacific and civil objects, will be a far more easy task than it has been to combine their physical powers to carry on extensive warlike operations.

The discovery of the distance and movements of the heavenly bodies; of the time-pieces; of a vessel to navigate the most distant parts of the ocean; of the steam engine, which performs, under the easy control of one man, the labour of many thousands; and of the press, by which knowledge and improvements may be speedily given to the most ignorant, in all parts of the earth;— these have, indeed, been discoveries of high import to mankind; but important as these and others have been in their effects, on the condition of human society, their combined benefits in practice, will fall far short of those which will be speedily attained by the new intellectual power, which men will acquire through the knowledge of "the science of the influence of circumstances over the whole conduct, character, and proceedings of the human race." By this latter discovery, more shall be accomplished in one year, for the well-being of human nature, including, without any exceptions, all ranks and descriptions of men, than has ever yet been effected in one or in many centuries. Strange as this language may seem to those whose minds have not yet had a glimpse of the real state in which society now is, it will prove to be not more strange than true.

Are not the mental energies of the world at this moment in a state of high effervescence? Is not society at a stand, incompetent to proceed in its present course, and do not all men cry out that "something must be done?" That "something," to produce the effect desired, must be a complete renovation of the whole social compact; one not forced on prematurely, by confusion and violence; not one to be brought about by the futile measures of the Radicals, Whigs, or Tories, of Britain,—the Liberals or Royalists of France,—the Illuminati of Germany, or the mere party proceedings of any little local portion of human beings, trained as they have hitherto been, in almost every kind of error, and without any true knowledge of themselves. No! The change sought for, must be preceded by the clear development of a great and universal principle which shall unite in one, all the petty jarring interests, by which, till now, nature has been made a most inveterate enemy to itself. No! extensive, nay, rather, universal as the re-arrangement of society must be, to relieve it from the difficulties with which it is now overwhelmed, it will be effected in peace and quietness, with the good will and hearty concurrence of all parties, and of every people. It will necessarily commence by common consent, on account of its advantages, almost simultaneously among all civilized nations; and, once begun, will daily advance with an accelerating ratio, unopposed, and bearing down before it the existing systems of the world. The only astonishment then will be that such systems could so long have existed. . . .

Under the present system, there is the most minute division of mental power and manual labour in the individuals of the working classes; private interests are placed perpetually at variance with the public good, and, in every nation, men are purposely trained from infancy to suppose, that their well-being is incompatible with the progress and prosperity of other nations. Such are the means by which old society seeks to obtain the desired effects of life. The details now to be submitted, have been devised upon principles which will lead to an opposite practice; to the combination of extensive mental and manual powers in the individuals of the working classes; to a complete identity of private and public interest, and to the training of nations to comprehend that their power and happiness cannot attain their full and natural development, but through an equal increase of the power and happiness of all other states. These, therefore, are the real points at variance between that which *is,* and that which *ought to be.*

It is upon these principles that arrangements are now proposed for the new agricultural villages, by which the food of the inhabitants may be prepared in one establishment, where they will eat together as one family. Various objects have been urged against this practice, but they have come from those only, who, whatever may be their pretensions in other respects, are mere children in the knowledge of the principle and economy of social life. By such arrangements, the members of these new associations may be supplied with food at far less expense, and with much more comfort, than by any individual or family arrangements; and when the parties have been once trained and accustomed, as they easily may be, to the former mode, they will never afterwards feel any inclination to return to the latter. If a saving in the quantity of food,—the obtaining of a superior quality of prepared provisions from the same materials,—and the operation of preparing them being effected in much less time, with far less fuel, and with greater ease, comfort, and health, to all the parties employed,—be advantages, these will be obtained in a remarkable manner by the new arrangements proposed. And if, to partake of viands so prepared, served up with every regard to comfort, in clean, spacious, well-lighted, and pleasantly-ventilated apartments, and in the society of well-dressed, well-trained, well-educated, and well-informed associates, possessing the most benevolent dispositions, and desirable habits, can give zest and proper enjoyment to meals, then will the inhabitants of the proposed villages experience all this in an eminent degree. . . .

We now proceed to describe the interior accommodations of the private lodging-houses which will occupy three sides of the parallelogram. As it is of essential importance that there should be abundance of space within the line of the private dwelling, the parallelogram, in all cases, whether the association is intended to be near the maximum or minimum in numbers, should be of large dimensions; and to accommodate a greater or less population, the private dwelling should be of one, two, three, or four storeys, and the interior arrangements formed accordingly. This will be very simple; no kitchen will be necessary, as the public arrangements for cooking will supersede the necessity for any. The apartments will be always well ventilated, and, when necessary, heated or cooled on the improved principles lately introduced in the Derby Infirmary. The expense and trouble, to say nothing of the superior health and comforts which these improvements will give, will be very greatly less than attach to the present practice. To heat, cool, and ventilate their apartments, the parties will have no further trouble than to open or shut two slides, or valves, in each room, the atmosphere of which, by this simple contrivance may be always kept temperate and pure. One stove of proper dimensions, judiciously placed, will supply the apartments of several dwellings with little trouble, and at a very light expense, when the buildings are originally adapted for this arrangement. Thus will all the inconveniences and expense of separate fires and fireplaces, and their appendages, be avoided, as well as the trouble and disagreeable effects of mending fires and removing ashes, &c. &c. Good sleeping apartments looking over the gardens into the country, and sitting-rooms of proper dimensions, fronting the square, will afford as much lodging-accommodation, as, with the other public arrangements, can be useful to, or desired by, these associated cultivators. . . .

Before any rational plan can be devised for the proper training and education of children, it should be distinctly known what capabilities and qualities infants and children possess, or, in fact, what they really are by nature. If this knowledge is to be attained, as all human knowledge has been acquired, through the evidence of the senses, then it is evident that infants receive, from a source and power over which they have no control, all the natural qualities they possess, and that from birth they are continually subjected to impressions derived from the circumstances around them; which impressions, combined with their natural qualities, whatever fanciful speculative men may say to the contrary, do truly determine the character of the individual through every period of life. . . .

It is reference to this important consideration, that your Reporter, in the forming of these new arrangements, has taken such pains to exclude every circumstance that could make an evil impression on the infants and children of this new generation. And he is prepared, when others can follow him, so to combine new circumstances, that real vice, or that conduct which creates evil and misery in society, shall be utterly unknown in these villages, to whatever number they may extend. Proceeding on these principles, your Reporter recommends arrangements, by which the children shall be trained together, as though they were literally

all of one family. For this purpose two schools will be required within the interior of the square, with spacious play and exercise ground. . . .

One of the most general sources of error and of evil in the world, is the notion *that infants, children, and men, are agents, governed by a will formed by themselves, and fashioned after their own choice.* It is, however, as evident as any fact can be made to man, that he does not possess the smallest control over the formation of any of his own faculties or powers, or over the peculiar and ever-varying manner in which those powers and faculties, physical and mental, are combined in each individual. Such being the case, it follows, that human nature, up to this period, has been misunderstood, vilified, and savagely ill treated; and that, in consequence, the language and conduct of mankind respecting it, form a compound of all that is inconsistent and incongruous, and most injurious to themselves, from the greatest to the least. All, at this moment, suffer grievously in consequence of this fundamental error. To those who possess any knowledge on this subject, it is known, that "man is a creature of circumstances," and that he really is, at every moment of his existence, precisely what the circumstances in which he has been placed, combined with his natural qualities, make him. . . . Surely if men ever become wise—if they ever acquire knowledge enough to know themselves, and enjoy a happy existence, it must be from discovering that they are not subjects for praise or blame, reward or punishment, but beings capable, by proper treatment, of receiving unlimited improvement and knowledge; and in consequence of experiencing such uninterrupted enjoyment through this life, as will best prepare them for an after-existence. . . .

The children in these new schools should be therefore trained systematically, to acquire useful knowledge through the means of sensible signs, by which their powers of reflection and judgment may be habituated to draw accurate conclusions from the facts presented to them. This mode of instruction is founded in nature, and will supersede the present defective and tiresome system of book learning, which is ill calculated to give either pleasure or instruction to the minds of children. When arrangements founded on these principles shall be judiciously formed and applied to practice, children will, with ease and delight to themselves, acquire more real knowledge in a day, then they have yet attained under the old system in many months. They will not only thus acquire valuable knowledge, but the best habits and dispositions will be at the same time imperceptibly created in every one; and they will be trained to fill every office, and to perform every duty, that the well-being of their associates and the establishments can require. It is only by education, rightly understood, that communities of men can ever be well governed, and by means of such education, every object of human society will be attained with the least labour, and the most satisfaction. . . .

But these associations must contribute their fair quota to the exigencies of the state. This consideration leads your Reporter to the next general head, or, The connection of the new establishments with the government of the country, and with old society.

Under this head are to be noticed, the amount and collection of the revenue, and the public or legal duties of the association in peace and war.

Your Reporter concludes, that whatever taxes are paid from land, capital, and labour, under the existing arrangements of society, the same amount for the same proportion of each may be collected with far more ease under those now proposed. The government would of course require its revenue to be paid in the legal circulating medium, to obtain which, the associations would have to dispose of as much of their surplus produce to common society for the legal coin or paper of the realm, as would discharge the demands of government. In time of peace, these associations would give no trouble to government, their internal regulations being founded on principle of prevention, not only with reference to public crimes, but to the private evils and errors which so fatally abound in common society. Courts of law, prisons, and punishments, would not be required. These are requisite only where human nature is greatly misunderstood; where society rests on the demoralizing system of individual rewards and punishments; —they are necessary only in a stage of existence previous to the discovery of the science of the certain and overwhelming influence of circumstances, over the whole character and conduct of mankind. Whatever courts of law, prisons, and punishments, have yet effected for society, the influence of other circumstances which may now be easily introduced, will accomplish infinitely more, for they will effectually prevent the growth of those evils, of which

our present Institutions do not take cognizance, till they are already full formed, and in baneful activity.

In time of peace, therefore, these associations will save much charge and trouble to government. In reference to war also, they will be equally beneficial. Bodily exercises, adapted to improve the dispositions, and increase the health and strength of the individual, will form part of the training and education of the children. In these exercises they may be instructed to acquire facility in the execution of combined movements, a habit which is calculated to produce regularity and order in time of peace, as well as to aid defensive and offensive operations in war. The children therefore, at an early age, will acquire *through their amusements* those habits which will render them capable of becoming, in a short time, at any future period of life, the best defenders of their country, if necessity should again arise to defend it, since they would in all probability be far more to be depended upon than those whose physical, intellectual, and moral training, had been less carefully conducted. In furnishing their quotas for the militia or common army, they would probably adopt the pecuniary alternative; by which means they would form a reserve, that, in proportion to their numbers, would be a great security for the nation's safety. They would prefer this alternative, to avoid the demoralizing effects of recruiting.

But the knowledge of the science of the influence of circumstances over mankind, will speedily enable all nations to discover, not only the evils of war, but the folly of it. Of all modes of conduct adopted by mankind to obtain advantages in the present stage of society, this is the most certain to defeat its object. It is, in truth, a system of demoralization and of destruction, while it is the highest interest of all individuals, and of all countries, to *remoralize and conserve.* Men surely cannot with truth be termed rational beings, until they shall discover and put in practice the principles which shall enable them to conduct their affairs without war. The arrangement we are considering, would speedily show how easily these principles and practices may be introduced into general society. . . .

. . . Possessing, in human nature, a soil capable of yielding abundantly the produce which man most desires, we have in our ignorance, planted the thorn instead of the vine. The evil principle, which has been instilled into all minds from infancy, "that the character is formed *by* the individual," has produced, and so long as it shall continue to be cherished, will ever produce, the unwelcome harvest of evil passions,—hatred, revenge, and all uncharitableness, and the innumerable crimes and miseries to which they have given birth; for these are the certain and necessary effects of the institutions which have arisen among mankind, in consequence of the universally received, and long coerced belief in this erroneous principle.

"That the character is formed *for* and not *by* the individual," is a truth to which every fact connected with man's history bears testimony, and of which the evidence of our senses affords us daily and hourly proof. It is also a truth which, when its practical application shall be fully understood, will be of inestimable value to mankind. Let us not, therefore, continue to act as if the reverse of this proposition were true. Let us cease to do violence to human nature; and having at length discovered the vine, or the good principle, let us henceforward substitute it for the thorn. The knowledge of this principle will necessarily lead to the gradual and peaceful introduction of other institutions and improved arrangements, which will preclude all the existing evils, and permanently secure the well-being and happiness of mankind. . . .

ETIENNE CABET (1788-1856)

Etienne Cabet is distinguished among nineteenth century socialists by his frank avowal of "Communist" principles. Elected to the French Chamber in 1831, he was forced to seek asylum in England from 1834 to 1839. There he came under the influence of Robert Owen. *Voyage to Icaria* (1840), the most popular of his works, was presented in the form of a novel describing the trip of an English traveler to Icaria, an ideal Communist state. Some of Cabet's disciples attempted to form such a society on the Red River in Texas, and Cabet, himself, led a similar group to Nauvoo, the former Mormon community, in Illinois. The first group made an epic, if fantastically stupid, overland trek from New Orleans to Texas. Both communities failed, and Cabet, one of many frustrated idealists drawn to the New World, died disconsolate at St. Louis, Missouri, in 1856.

The selections that follow are from *Voyage en Icarie* and a short pamphlet, *Credo Communist* (translations by the editors).

VOYAGE TO ICARIA (1840)

CHAPTER II

ARRIVAL IN ICARIA

I left London the 22nd of December 1835, and I arrived the 24th of April with my good John, the faithful companion of my travels, at the port of Camaris on the east coast of the country of the Marvols, separated from Icaria by an arm of the sea that one can cross in six hours.

I shall not recount the thousand accidents that occurred along the way: robbed in almost all the hostels; almost poisoned in one; persecuted by the police or authorities; vexed and outraged by the customs officials; arrested and imprisoned for several days for protesting the insolence of one of them; often threatened with being shaken apart, along with the conveyance, by the wretched condition of the roads; miraculously saved from falling over a precipice where we were thrown by a miserable coachman who was blind drunk; almost buried in snow and then in sand; three times attacked by robbers; wounded between two travelers who were killed at my side; I experienced an inexpressible joy on finding myself at the end of my journey.

I was even happier when, meeting some Icarians, I discovered that I could understand and speak the Icarian language to which I had devoted all my time on the journey.

I went directly to the consulate and was admitted at once.

The consul received me with a good will that appeared totally lacking in affectation, and he asked me to take a chair by him.

—If your purpose, he told me, is to purchase goods, do not go to Icaria; for we *do not sell anything;* if you came only to sell, stop now; for we *do not buy anything;* but if your only purpose is curiosity, you may continue; your trip will be a pleasant one.

I kept repeating to myself with astonishment, they sell nothing, they buy nothing! . . .

Principles of Social Organization in Icaria

You know, he said, that man is distinguished from all other animate beings by his *reason,* his *perfectibility* and his *sociability.*

The Icarians, profoundly convinced through experience, that man cannot have happiness without association and equality have joined together in a *society* founded on the basis of the most perfect *equality.* All are *associates, citizens, equals* in rights and duties; all share equally the burdens and the benefits of the association; all also form but a single *family* whose members are united by ties of *fraternity.*

We form then a *People* or a *Nation* of brothers, and all our laws must have for their purpose the establishing among us of an absolute equality in all cases except those where equality is manifestly impossible.

—Yet, I said, has not *nature* itself established inequality by almost always giving men unequal physical and mental powers?

—That is true, he replied, but also is it not nature that has given men the same desire to be happy, the same love of equality, the intelligence and *reason* with which to organize happiness, society and equality?

—Besides, sir, don't stop with that objection, for we have resolved the problem, and you will have an opportunity to witness the most complete *social equality.*

Just as we have formed a single society, people, family, our land, with its mines below the surface and all structures above ground, forms a single *domain* which is our common domain.

All the property of the associates, together with all the products of the land and industry form but one common *capital.*

This common domain and common property belong indivisibly to the people who together cultivate and utilize them, who administer them either directly or through elected officials, and who likewise share equally in all the benefits from them.

—But, that means *community of Goods!* I cried.—Precisely, . . . does this Community frighten you?—No . . . but . . . they have always said it was impossible — Impossible! you will see. . . .

The Icarians, being associates and equals, must all follow a trade and work the same number of hours; but all their intelligence is directed toward finding every possible means of making work short, varied, pleasant and free from danger.

All tools and materials are provided from the common fund, just as all products of the land and industry are consigned to public warehouses.

All of us are nourished, clothed, lodged and provided with furnishings from the common fund, and we are all treated *the same,* according to sex, age and other circumstances foreseen by the law of the land.

Thus it is the Republic or the Community which alone is proprietor of everything, which organizes its workers, and which constructs its shops and warehouses; it is it that provides for tilling the land; that builds the houses; that manufactures all things necessary to nourishment, clothing, lodging and furnishings. . . .

Education being considered among us as the foundation of society, the Republic provides it for all children and provides it to them equally, just as it likewise nourishes all equally. All receive the same primary schooling and a special training appropriate to any particular profession; and this education has as its object the forming of good workers, good parents, good citizens and *real* men.

In substance, such is our social organization, and from these few words you can divine the rest.

You can understand now why we have neither *poor* nor *domestics.*

You must understand also why it is that the Republic owns all the horses, carriages, hotels that you have seen and why it feeds and transports travelers free of charge.

You must likewise understand that, since each of us receives in kind all that is needed, *money, purchase* and *sale* are completely useless to us.

Yes, I replied, I understand very well . . . But . . .

COMMUNIST CREED (1841)

Nature.—I do not believe that the Universe can be the product of accident; but I believe in a *First Cause* which I call *Nature.*

I believe it to be *useless* and *dangerous* to insist on characterizing this *First Cause,* because human intelligence is not perfect enough to perceive and know it, and because any discussion on this point usually degenerates into *disputes* and *divisions.* But I believe Nature is infinitely intelligent and farsighted, infinitely powerful and wise, infinitely *just* and *benevolent.*

Happiness.—I believe that Nature intended that Man should be *happy* on Earth.

I believe that all the objects that it has created around him, the organization that it has given him, and especially Intelligence or Reason, suffice for him to discover *Happiness.*

I believe that if Man is unhappy, it is not due to any intention of Nature, but is the effect of the ignorance of the human race at birth, of its inexperience and first errors, of the faulty institutions it designed, of the bad *social and political Organisation* introduced in a period of barbarism. . . .

Reason.—I believe man is essentially *reasonable, perfectible, sociable.*

I believe the number of men whose reason could be corrupted, when developed by a good Education and a good social Organization, to be infinitesimally, small.

But I believe that Intelligence or *Reason,* which distinguishes Man from all other animate beings, suffices, when enlightened by Experience, for perfecting Humanity.

Perfectibility.—I believe that Man is essentially *perfectible* by Experience and by Education; that the human race from its birth to the present has been generally and constantly perfecting itself; that it is more instructed than in any former time; and that it is impossible to fix the limits to its future perfection.

Sociability.—I believe that man is essentially *sociable;* that he is destined to live in Society; that in greater or lesser numbers he has always and everywhere existed in Society; that Society is *natural;* and that what they call *civil* or *political* Society is only the continuation, the development and the perfecting of *natural* Society, aided by Reason and by Experience.

Natural Goodness.—I believe that man, being essentially *sociable,* is basically *attracted* toward his kind, and is *sympathetic,*

compassionate, affectionate, good, disposed to succour and aid his fellow men; that *fraternity, love, devotion,* are natural dispositions or instincts that are confirmed and developed by Reason and Education.

I believe that the vices of men are generally the effect of bad social and political organization, and especially of *Inequality,* which produces egoism and indifference, envy and hatred.

I believe that if Equality replaces Inequality in the social and political Organization all vices will disappear and give way before fraternity, love, devotion.

Fraternity—I believe that Nature is the common *mother* of men, that all men are equally her *children,* that all are *brothers,* and that the human race . . . forms only *one family.*

I believe that Nature has not divided its children into castes, classes, races, corporations, categories; that it has not destined *some* to be masters, governors, rich, lazy, enjoying all privileges, without responsibility, happy, living in superfluity, and *others* to be slaves, governed, poor, burdened with labor, bearing all taxes, without enjoyment of any advantage, unhappy, deprived of necessities.

I believe on the contrary that the *Fraternity* of men necessarily carries with it their *Equality.*

Equality—I believe that *differences* in height, form, strength, etc. in no way prevent *Equality in rights, in duties, in happiness,* just as differences between children do not prevent them enjoying the same right to the love of their parents, or as the differences among citizens do not prevent their equality in the eyes of the law and the tribunals.

I believe that Nature has created everything found on earth for the benefit of the human Race, *all for all;* that it has given the same needs to all and consequently the same rights to the things needed to satisfy them; . . . that it has given its heritage to all *in common;* and that it has given to each one an equal right to the land and all its products, just as to the air, light and heat.

I do not believe that Nature gave man Reason and made him sociable in order that Reason and Society should destroy Fraternity and Equality of rights. I believe on the contrary that it created man reasonable, perfectible and sociable in order that Reason and Society might perfect and realize *Equality* in happiness.

I believe that the establishment of social and political Inequality is a violation of natural Law.

I believe that this social and political Inequality was established among all Nations only because the human Race began by being brutalized and completely ignorant.

I do not believe that the true or sole cause of the misfortunes of people is *Monarchy,* and that the true remedy is the *Republic,* for History shows us evils in the Republics as well as in the Monarchies.

I believe that Inequality which produces opulence and domination for the minority, *misery* and *oppression* for the majority of the human Race, is the root *cause* of all the vices of the rich (egoism, cupidity, ambition, avarice, insensibility and inhumanity) and of all the vices of the poor (jealousy, envy, hatred).

I believe that it is also the cause of rivalries and antagonism, of all disorders and discords, of conspiracies and insurrections, of all crimes and calamaties.

I believe that the same *effects* will continue so long as the *cause* persists, and that the sole means of ending the misfortunes of Humanity is to suppress Aristrocracy or social and political Inequality by replacing it with Democracy or Equality.

Property.—I believe that Nature destined the earth to be held in *common* and *indivisibly,* like the air, light and heat; that it intended only a division of the fruits of the earth and of objects necessary to each person; and that *Community* of goods is *natural.*

I believe that *Property* is a purely human invention and institution.

I believe that this institution can be good and useful only to the degree to which the land is divided among all men so that each has an equal part and this part must be essentially inalienable.

I believe that that the institution of Property, combined with Inequality and inalienability, as practiced among almost all Nations, is an *error* and perhaps one of the most fateful of all errors.

I believe that unlimited Property has facilitated Inequality of fortunes, and that it is the principal cause of opulence and misery, of all vices, of all misfortunes of Humanity.

I believe that these misfortunes will continue essentially, fatally, inevitably, so long as Property continues; and that if one wants the *effect* to cease one must necessarily remove the *cause.*

I believe that instead of the *opulence* of the few and the *misery* of the great majority it is necessary to establish the *well-being* of all; and I believe that in order to establish this universal well-being it is necessary to reestablish the *natural Community* of goods while perfecting it.

ORGANIZATION OF THE COMMUNITY

People in the community.—I believe that the Nation or the People should form a single *Family* of brothers or a single Society whose members would be equal in rights and duties, in enjoyment and labor.

I believe that Equality should be perfect and have no other limit than the possible.

I believe that all brothers or associates should be equally citizens, electors, eligibles; that all should receive the same elementary and general education; that all should be equally well nourished, clothed and lodged; that all should be equally subject to the law; and that all should work equally. . . .

Law.—I believe that Law should be the expression of the general will; that it can be prepared by a popular Representation elected by all citizens; but that it must, so far as possible, be approved by the entire People.

I believe that when the Law is thus made by all, consented and willed by all, it necessarily is in the interest of all, and that no one can experience the slightest objection to executing Law that is agreed to by each person as being in the common interest. . . .

Industry in the community.—I believe that all branches of industry should form but a *single social Industry* directed by a single will.

I believe that it is Society that must apportion and direct the *work,* organize and locate the shops, distribute all the workers.

I believe that each *shop* should be specialized, combine all workers of a single skill, and produce each product in enormous quantity.

I believe that *machines,* often disastrous to the poor under the present system, cannot be carried too far under the system of the Community; that all work that is burdensome, dangerous, unpleasant, should be executed by machines; and that all human ingenuity should be directed toward discovering means by which the role of men shall be limited to operating machines.

I believe that everything should be done to make work *easy* and *agreeable*.

I believe that, with all labor equally ordered by Society, all should be given equal *consideration*.

I believe that all citizens should be *workers;* that each should, so far as possible, choose that profession that most pleases him; gives him the most pleasure and that all should work at *the same time*.

I believe that the result of this industrial system will be to avoid much *duplicate effort* and numerous *losses,* will realize immense *economies,* and will bring a ten-fold increase in *manufacture*.

Happy effects of the community.—I believe that this system of Communal living, giving a *good education and leisure* to all, will put an end to all *disorders,* all *vices,* all *crimes,* and will assure the most perfect *public order, peace* and *happiness* for *all citizens*.

I believe that, far from leading to *Equality of misery,* the Community will lead to *Equality of leisure*. . . .

I believe that, under the Community, there will be neither thieves, nor drunkards, nor idle; that trials and bankruptcies will be unknown; that courts, penalties, prisons, police, etc. will be useless.

Possibility of application.—I believe the opinion that rejects the Community as impossible, as a fantasy, as an utopia, is only a *prejudice* and *hindrance* that will evaporate before study and examination.

I believe moreover that the Community, being in need of great productive force and creativity to provide equality of leisure, is more practical in a great industrial and commercial nation than in a petty state without industry; that it is easier today than in any former period, for industry today is more powerful than ever before; and that with each year it will become more realizable.

Establishment of the community.—I do not believe that the Community can be established through *violence,* nor that a victorious minority can force it upon the majority.

I believe that if a minority should try to suppress property, in face of the opposition of the small and large landholders, and force the present wealthy class to work, this enterprise, which would constitute a break with all habits and overturn all existing patterns, would encounter more obstacles than any social or political change yet attempted.

I believe that independent of the resistance taking the form of overt force, the resistance by *force of inertia* would suffice to make the attempt fail.

I believe that the Community can be established solely by the force of *public opinion,* by the national will, by the consent of all or of a great majority, in a word by Law.

I believe that to form this public opinion, national will, consent, majority, it is necessary to *discuss,* reassure, lead, persuade, convince, adopt. . . .

I believe that menace and violence would have a *counter-effect;* that the Communists must prove the superiority of their doctrine by their tolerance and moderation, by their benevolence and fraternity toward all men, and especially toward those who march with a more or less rapid step along the path of reform and progress. . . .

I believe that to smooth away the difficulties, it is necessary to satisfy the present adversaries by *sincerely* announcing that the present Generation will neither be stripped of its rights to property nor forced to work, and that the system of the Community will become obligatory only for the new-born Generation which will be prepared for it by education. . . .

All these principles are developed in our *Voyage to Icaria* which shows a *great Nation organized into a Community.*

KARL MARX (1818-1883)

AND

FRIEDRICH ENGELS (1820-1895)

The names of Karl Marx and Friedrich Engels deserve to be linked together. Although Engels was definitely the junior partner and constantly effaced himself, recent scholars give him credit for sizeable portions of works once wholly attributed to Marx. Both were Germans, born in the Rhineland of substantial middle-class families. Marx studied philosophy at Bonn and the University of Berlin where his views brought him into trouble with the authorities. In 1843 he fled to Paris, then to Brussels and London, where he spent most of his life working in the British Museum on his great treatise, *Das Capital*. Engels was sent to England to manage a family mill near Manchester. He participated in the Chartist agitation and was at work on a book, *The Condition of the Working Class in England,* before meeting Marx in 1844. Thereafter the two remained intimate friends and collaborators. Engels edited the second and third volumes of *Capital*. *The Communist Manifesto,* although only a pamphlet, is an epitome of Marxian Socialism.

PREFACE TO THE 1888 EDITION OF THE MANIFESTO

The "Manifesto" was published as the platform of the "Communist League," a working-men's association, first exclusively German, later on international, and, under the political conditions of the Continent before 1848, unavoidably a secret society. At a Congress of the League, held in London in November, 1847, Marx and Engels were commissioned to prepare for publication a complete theoretical and practical party-programme. Drawn up in German, in January, 1848, the manuscript was sent to the printer in London a few weeks before the French revolution of February 24th. A French translation was brought out in Paris, shortly before the insurrection of June, 1848. The first English translation, by Miss Helen Macfarlane, appeared in . . . London, 1850. . . .

When it was written, we could not have called it a *Socialist*

Manifesto. By Socialist, in 1847, were understood, on the one hand, the adherents of the various Utopian systems: Owenites in England, Fourierists in France, both of them already reduced to the position of mere sects, and gradually dying out; on the other hand, the most multifarious social quacks, who, by all manner of tinkering, professed to redress, without any danger to capital and profit, all sorts of social grievances—in both cases men outside the working class movement, and looking rather to the "educated" classes for support. Whatever portion of the working class had become convinced of the insufficiency of mere political revolutions, and had proclaimed the necessity of a total social change, that portion then, called itself Communist. It was a crude, rough-hewn, purely instinctive sort of Communism; still, it touched the cardinal point and was powerful enough amongst the working class to produce the Utopian Communism, in France, of Cabet, and in Germany, of Weitling. Thus, Socialism was, in 1847, a middle-class movement, Communism a working-class movement. Socialism was, on the Continent at least "respectable;" Communism was the very opposite. And as our notion, from the very beginning, was that "the emancipation of the working class must be the act of the working class itself," there could be no doubt as to which of the two names we must take. Moreover, we have, ever since, been far from repudiating it.

The "Manifesto" being our joint production, I consider my-self bound to state that the fundamental proposition which forms its nucleus belongs to Marx. That proposition is: that in every historical epoch, the prevailing mode of economic production and exchange, and the social organisation necessarily following from it, form the bases upon which is built up, and from which alone can be explained, the political and intellectual history of that epoch; that consequently the whole history of mankind (since the dissolution of primitive tribal society, holding land in common ownership) has been a history of class struggles, contests between exploiting and exploited, ruling and oppressed classes; that the history of these class struggles form a series of evolution in which, now-a-days, a stage has been reached where the exploited and oppressed class—the proletariat—cannot attain its emancipation from the sway of the exploiting and ruling class—the bourgeoisie without at the same time, and once and for all emancipating society at large from all exploitation, oppression, class-distinctions and class-struggles.

This proposition, in my opinion, is destined to do for history what Darwin's theory has done for biology. . . .

The present translation is by Mr. Samuel Moore, the translator of the greater portion of Marx's "Capital." We have revised it in common, and I have added a few notes* explanatory of historical allusions.

London, 30th January, 1888

*(Engels' notes have been omitted.)

MANIFESTO OF THE COMMUNIST PARTY (1848)

A spectre is haunting Europe—the spectre of Communism. All the powers of old Europe have entered into a holy alliance to exorcise this spectre; Pope and Czar, Metternich and Guizot, French Radicals and German police-spies.

Where is the party in opposition that has not been decried as communistic by its opponents in power? Where the Opposition that has not hurled back the branding reproach of Communism, against the more advanced opposition parties, as well as against its reactionary adversaries,

Two things result from this fact.

I. Communism is already acknowledged by all European Powers to be itself a Power.

II. It is high time that Communists should openly, in the face of the whole world, publish their views, their aims, their tendencies, and meet this nursery tale of the Spectre of Communism with a Manifesto of the party itself.

To this end, Communists of various nationalities have assembled in London, and sketched the following manifesto, to be published in the English, French, German, Italian, Flemish and Danish languages.

I. BOURGEOIS AND PROLETARIANS

The history of all hitherto existing society is the history of class struggles.

Freeman and slave, patrician and plebeian, lord and serf, guild-master and journeyman, in a word, oppressor and oppressed, stood in constant opposition to one another, carried on an uninterrupted, now hidden, now open fight, a fight that each time ended, either in a revolutionary re-constitution of society at large, or in the common ruin of the contending classes.

In the earlier epochs of history, we find almost everywhere a complicated arrangement of society into various orders, a manifold graduation of social rank. In ancient Rome we have patricians, knights, plebeians, slaves; in the middle ages, feudal lords, vassals, guild-masters, journeymen, apprentices, serfs; in almost all of these classes, again, subordinate gradations.

The modern bourgeois society that has sprouted from the ruins of feudal society, has not done away with class antagonisms. It has but established new classes, new conditions of oppression, new forms of struggle in place of the old ones.

Our epoch, the epoch of the bourgeoisie, possesses, however, this distinctive feature; it has simplified the class antagonisms. Society as a whole is more and more splitting up into two great hostile camps, into two great classes directly facing each other: Bourgeoisie and Proletariat.

From the serfs of the middle ages sprang the chartered burghers of the earliest towns. From these burgesses the first elements of the bourgeoisie were developed.

The discovery of America, the rounding of the Cape, opened up fresh ground for the rising bourgeoisie. The East-Indian and Chinese markets, the colonization of America, trade with the colonies, the increase in the means of exchange and in commodities generally, gave to commerce, to navigation, to industry, an impulse never before known, and thereby, to the revolutionary element in the tottering feudal society, a rapid development.

The feudal system of industry, under which industrial production was monopolized by close guilds, now no longer sufficed for the growing wants of the new markets. The manufacturing system took its place. The guild-masters were pushed on one side by the manufacturing middle-class; division of labor between the different corporate guilds vanished in the face of division of labor in each single workshop.

Meantime the markets kept ever growing, the demand, ever rising. Even manufacture no longer sufficed. Thereupon, steam and machinery revolutionized industrial production. The place of manufacture was taken by the giant, Modern Industry, the place of the industrial middle-class, by industrial millionaires, the leaders of whole industrial armies, the modern bourgeois.

Modern industry has established the world-market, for which the discovery of America paved the way. This market has given an immense development to commerce, to navigation, to communication by land. This development has, in its turn, reacted on the extension of industry; and in proportion as industry, commerce, navigation, railways extended, in the same proportion the bourgeoisie developed, increased its capital, and pushed into the background every class handed down from the Middle Ages.

We see, therefore, how the modern bourgeoisie is itself the product of a long course of development, of a series of revolutions in the modes of production and of exchange.

Each step in the development of the bourgeoisie was accompanied by a corresponding political advance of that class. An oppressed class under the sway of the feudal nobility, an armed and self-governing association in the mediaeval commune, here independent urban republic (as in Italy and Germany), there taxable "third estate" of the monarchy (as in France), afterwards, in the period of manufacture proper, serving either the semi-feudal or the absolute monarchy as a counterpoise against the nobility, and, in fact, cornerstone of the great monarchies in general, the bourgeoisie has at last since the establishment of Modern Industry and of the world-market, conquered for itself, in the modern representative State, exclusive political sway. The executive of the modern state is but a committee for managing the common affairs of the whole bourgeoisie.

The bourgeoisie, historically, has played a most revolutionary part.

The bourgeoisie, wherever it has got the upper hand, has put an end to all feudal, patriarchal, idyllic relations. It has pitilessly torn asunder the motley feudal ties that bound man to his "natural superiors," and has left remaining no other nexus between man and man than naked self-interest, than callous "cash payment." It has drowned the most heavenly ecstasies of religious fervor, of chivalrous enthusiasm, of philistine sentimentalism, in the icy water of egotistical calculation. It has resolved personal worth into exchange value, and in place of the numberless indefeasible chartered freedoms, has set up that single, unconscionable freedom—Free Trade. In one word, for exploitation, veiled by religious and political illusions, it has substituted naked, shameless, direct, brutal exploitation.

The bourgeoisie has stripped of its halo every occupation

hitherto honored and looked up to with reverent awe. It has converted the physician, the lawyer, the priest, the poet, the man of science, into its paid wage-laborers.

The bourgeoisie has torn away from the family its sentimental veil, and has reduced the family relation to a mere money relation.

The bourgeoisie has disclosed how it came to pass that the brutal display of vigor in the Middle Ages, which Reactionists so much admire, found its fitting complement in the most slothful indolence. It has been the first to show what man's activity can bring about. It has accomplished wonders far surpassing Egyptian pyramids, Roman aqueducts, and Gothic cathedrals; it has conducted expeditions that put in the shade all former Exoduses of nations and crusades.

The bourgeoisie cannot exist without constantly revolutionizing the instruments of production, and thereby the relations of production, and with them the whole relations of society. Conservation of the old modes of production in unaltered form, was on the contrary, the first condition of existence for all earlier industrial classes. Constant revolutionizing of production, uninterrupted disturbance of all social conditions, everlasting uncertainty and agitation distinguish the bourgeois epoch from all earlier ones. All fixed, fast-frozen relations, with their train of ancient and venerable prejudices and opinions, are swept away, all new-formed ones become antiquated before they can ossify. All that is solid melts into air, all that is holy is profaned, and man is at last compelled to face, with sober senses, his real conditions of life, and his relations with his kind.

The need of a constantly expanding market for its products chases the bourgeoisie over the whole surface of the globe. It must nestle everywhere, settle everywhere, establish connections everywhere.

The bourgeoisie has through its exploitation of the world-market given a cosmopolitan character to production and consumption in every country. To the great chagrin of Reactionists, it has drawn from under the feet of industry the national ground on which it stood. All old-established national industries have been destroyed or are daily being destroyed. They are dislodged by new industries, whose introduction becomes a life and death question for all civilized nations, by industries that no longer work up indigenous raw material, but raw material drawn from the remotest zones; industries whose products are consumed, not only at home, but in every quarter of the globe. In place of the old wants, satisfied by the productions of the country, we find new wants, requiring for their satisfaction the products of distant lands and climes. In place of the old local and national seclusion and self-sufficiency, we have intercourse in every direction, universal inter-dependence of nations. And as in material, so also in intellectual production. The intellectual creations of individual nations become common property. National one-sidedness and narrow-mindedness become more and more impossible, and from the numerous national and local literatures there arises a world-literature.

The bourgeoisie, by the rapid improvement of all instruments of production, by the immensely facilitated means of communication, draws all, even the most barbarian, nations into civilization. The cheap prices of its commodities are the heavy artillery with which it batters down all Chinese walls, with which it forces the barbarians' intensely obstinate hatred of foreigners to capitulate. It compels all nations, on pain of extinction, to adopt the bourgeois mode of production; it compels them to introduce what it calls civilization into their midst, i.e., to become bourgeois themselves. In a word, it creates a world after its own image.

The bourgeoisie has subjected the country to the rule of the towns. It has created enormous cities, has greatly increased the urban population as compared with the rural, and has thus rescued a considerable part of the population from the idiocy of rural life. Just as it has made the country dependent on the towns, so it has made barbarian and semi-barbarian countries dependent on the civilized ones, nations of peasants on nations of bourgeois, the East on the West.

The bourgeoisie keeps more and more doing away with the scattered state of the population, of the means of production, and of property. It has agglomerated population, centralized means of production, and has concentrated property in a few hands. The necessary conseqence of this was political centralization. Independent, or but loosely connected provinces, with separate interests, laws, governments and systems of taxation, became lumped together in one nation, with one government, one code of laws, one national class-interest, one frontier and one customs-tariff.

The bourgeoisie, during its rule of scarce one hundred years, has created more massive and more colossal productive forces than have all preceding generations together. Subjection of Nature's forces to man, machinery, application of chemistry to industry and agriculture, steam-navigation, railways, electric telegraphs, clearing of whole continents for cultivation, canalization of rivers, whole populations conjured out of the ground—what earlier century had even a presentiment that such productive forces slumbered in the lap of social labor?

We see then: the means of production and of exchange on whose foundation the bourgeoisie built itself up, were generated in feudal society. At a certain stage in the development of these means of production and of exchange, the conditions under which feudal society produced and exchanged, the feudal organization of agriculture and manufacturing industry, in one word, the feudal relations of property became no longer compatible with the already developed productive forces; they became so many fetters. They had to burst asunder; they were burst asunder.

Into their places stepped free competition, accompanied by a social and political constitution adapted to it, and by the economical and political sway of the bourgeois class.

A similar movement is going on before our own eyes. Modern bourgeois society with its relations of production, of exchange and of property, a society that has conjured up such gigantic means of production and of exchange, is like the sorcerer, who is no longer able to control the powers in the nether world whom he has called up by his spells. For many a decade past the history of industry and commerce is but the history of the revolt of modern productive forces against modern conditions of production, against the property relations that are the conditions for the existence of the bourgeoisie and of its rule. It is enough to mention the commercial crises that by their periodical return put on its trial, each time more threateningly, the existence of the entire bourgeois society. In these crises a great part not only of the existing products, but also of the previously created productive forces, are periodically destroyed. In these crises there breaks out an epidemic that, in all earlier epochs, would have seemed an absurdity—the epidemic of over-production. Society suddenly finds itself put back into a state of momentary barbarism; it appears as if a famine, a universal war of devastation had cut off the supply of every means of subsistence; industry and commerce seem to be destroyed; and why? Because there is too much civilization, too much means of subsistence, too much industry, too much commerce. The productive forces at the disposal of society no longer tend to further the development of the conditions of bourgeois property; on the contrary, they have become too powerful for these conditions, by which they are fettered, and so soon as they overcome these fetters, they bring disorder into the whole of bourgeois society, endanger the existence of bourgeois property. The conditions of bourgeois society are too narrow to comprise the wealth created by them. And how does the bourgeoisie get over these crises? On the one hand by enforced destruction of a mass of productive forces; on the other, by the conquest of new markets, and by the more thorough exploitation of the old ones. That is to say, by paving the way for more extensive and more destructive crises, and by diminishing the means whereby crises are prevented.

The weapons with which the bourgeoisie felled feudalism to the ground are now turned against the bourgeoisie itself.

But not only has the bourgeoisie forged the weapons that bring death to itself; it has also called into existence the men who are to wield those weapons—the modern working-class—the proletarians.

In proportion as the bourgeoisie, i.e., capital, is developed, in the same proportion is the proletariat, the modern working-class, developed, a class of laborers, who live only so long as they find work, and who find work only so long as their labor increases capital. These laborers, who must sell themselves piecemeal, are a commodity, like every other article of commerce, and are consequently exposed to all the vicissitudes of competition, to all the fluctuations of the market.

Owing to the extensive use of machinery and to division of labor, the work of the proletarians has lost all individual character, and, consequently, all charm for the workman. He becomes an appendage of the machine, and it is only the most simple, most monotonous, and most easily acquired knack that is required of him. Hence, the cost of production of a workman is restricted, almost entirely, to the means of subsistence that he requires for his maintenance, and for the propagation of his race. But the price of a commodity, and also of labor, is equal to its cost of production. In proportion, therefore, as the repulsiveness of the work increases, the wage decreases. Nay more, in proportion as the use of machinery and division of labor increases, in the same proportion the burden of toil also increases, whether by prolongation of the working hours, by increase of the work enacted in a given time, or by increased speed of the machinery, etc.

Modern industry has converted the little workshop of the patriarchal master into the great factory of the industrial capitalist. Masses of laborers, crowded into the factory, are organized like soldiers. As privates of the industrial army they are placed under the command of a perfect heirarchy of officers and sergeants. Not only are they the slaves of the bourgeois class, and of the bourgeois State, they are daily and hourly enslaved by the machine, by the over-looker, and, above all, by the individual bourgeois manufacturer himself. The more openly this despotism proclaims gain to be its end and aim, the more petty, the more hateful and the more embittering it is.

The less the skill and exertion or strength implied in manual labor, in other words, the more modern industry becomes developed, the more is the labor of men superseded by that of women. Differences of age and sex have no longer any distinctive social validity for the working class. All are instruments of labor, more or less expensive to use, according to their age and sex.

No sooner is the exploitation of the laborer by the manufacturer, so far at an end, that he receives his wages in cash, than he is set upon by the other portions of the bourgeoisie, the landlord, the shopkeeper, the pawnbroker, etc.

The lower strata of the middle class—the small tradespeople, shopkeepers, and retired tradesmen generally, the handicraftsmen and peasants—all these sink gradually into the proletariat, partly because their diminutive capital does not suffice for the scale on which Modern Industry is carried on, and is swamped in the competition with the large capitalists, partly because their specialized skill is rendered worthless by new methods of production. Thus the proletariat is recruited from all classes of the population.

The proletariat goes through various stages of development. With its birth begins its struggle with the bourgeoisie. At first the contest is carried on by individual laborers, then by the workpeople of a factory, then by the operatives of one trade, in one locality, against the individual bourgeois who directly exploits them. They direct their attacks not against the bourgeois conditions of production, but against the instruments of production themselves; they destroy imported wares that compete with their labor, they smash to pieces machinery, they set factories ablaze, they seek to restore by force the vanished status of the workman of the Middle Ages.

At this stage the laborers still form an incoherent mass scattered over the whole country, and broken up by their mutual competition. If anywhere they unite to form more compact bodies, this is not yet the consequence of their own active union, but of the union of the bourgeoisie, which class, in order to attain its own political ends, is compelled to set the whole proletariat in motion, and is moreover yet, for a time, able to do so. At this stage, therefore, the proletarians do not fight their enemies, but the enemies of their enemies, the remnants of absolute monarchy, the landowners, the non-industrial bourgeois, the petty bourgeoisie. Thus the whole historical movement is concentrated in the hands of the bourgeoisie; every victory so obtained is a victory for the bourgeoisie.

But with the development of industry the proletariat not only increases in number, it becomes concentrated in greater masses, its strength grows, and it feels that strength more. The various interests and conditions of life within the ranks of the proletariat are more and more equalized, in proportion as machinery obliterates all distinctions of labor, and nearly everywhere reduces wages to the same low level. The growing competition among the bourgeois, and the resulting commercial crises, make the wages of the workers ever more fluctuating. The unceasing improvement of machinery, ever more rapidly developing, makes their livelihood more and more precarious; the collisions between individual workmen and individual bourgeois take more and more the character of collisions between two classes. Thereupon the workers begin to form combinations (Trades' Unions) against the bourgeois; they club together in order to keep up the rate of wages; they found permanent associations in order to make provision beforehand for these occasional revolts. Here and there the contest breaks out into riots.

Now and then the workers are victorious, but only for a

time. The real fruit of their battle lies, not in the immediate result, but in the ever-expanding union of the workers. This union is helped on by the improved means of communication that are created by modern industry, and that place the workers of different localities in contact with one another. It was just this contact that was needed to centralize the numerous local struggles, all of the same character, into one national struggle between classes. But every class struggle is a political struggle. And that union, to attain which the burghers of the Middle Ages, with their miserable highways, required centuries, the modern proletarians, thanks to railways, achieve in a few years.

This organization of the proletarians into a class, and consequently into a political party, is continually being upset again by the competition between the workers themselves. But it ever rises up again, stronger, firmer, mightier. It compels legislative recognition of particular interest of the workers, by taking advantage of the divisions among the bourgeoisie itself. Thus the ten-hour bill in England was carried.

Altogether collisions between the classes of the old society further, in many ways, the course of development of the proletariat. The bourgeoisie finds itself involved in a constant battle. At first with the aristocracy; later on, with those portions of the bourgeoisie itself, whose interests have become antagonistic to the progress of industry; at all times, with the bourgeoisie of foreign countries. In all these battles it sees itself compelled to appeal to the proletariat, to ask for its help, and thus, to drag it into the political arena. The bourgeoisie itself, therefore, supplies the proletariat with its own elements of political and general education, in other words, it furnishes the proletariat with weapons for fighting the bourgeoisie.

Further, as we have already seen, entire sections of the ruling classes are, by the advance of industry, precipitated into the proletariat, or are at least threatened in their conditions of existence. These also supply the proletariat with fresh elements of enlightenment and progress.

Finally, in times when the class-struggle nears the decisive hour, the process of dissolution going on within the ruling class, in fact, within the whole range of old society, assumes such a violent, glaring character, that a small section of the ruling class cuts itself adrift, and joins the revolutionary class, the class that holds the future in its hands. Just as, therefore, at an earlier period, a section of the nobility went over to the bourgeoisie, so now a portion of the bourgeoisie goes over to the proletariat, and in particular, a portion of the bourgeois ideologists, who have raised themselves to the level of comprehending theoretically the historical movements as a whole.

Of all the classes that stand face to face with the bourgeoisie today, the proletariat alone is a really revolutionary class. The other classes decay and finally disappear in the face of modern industry; the proletariat is its special and essential product.

The lower middle-class, the small manufacturer, the shopkeeper, the artisan, the peasant, all these fight against the bourgeoisie, to save from extinction their existence as fractions of the middle class. They are, therefore, not revolutionary, but conservative. Nay more, they are reactionary, for they try to roll back the wheel of history. If by chance they are revolutionary, they are so, only in view of their impending transfer into the proletariat, they thus defend not their present, but their future interests, they desert their own standpoint to place themselves at that of the proletariat.

The "dangerous class," the social scum, that passively rotting mass thrown off by the lowest layers of old society, may, here and there be swept into the movement by a proletarian revolution; its conditions of life, however, prepare it far more for the part of a bribed tool of reactionary intrigue.

In the conditions of the proletariat, those of old society at large are already virtually swamped. The proletarian is without property; his relation to his wife and children has no longer anything in common with the bourgeois family-relations; modern industrial labor, modern subjection to capital, the same in England as in France, in America as in Germany, has stripped him of every trace of national character. Law, morality, religion, are to him so many bourgeois prejudices, behind which lurk in ambush just as many bourgeois interests.

All the preceding classes that got the upper hand, sought to fortify their already acquired status by subjecting society at large to their conditions of appropriation. The proletarians cannot become masters of the productive forces of society, except by abolishing their own previous mode of appropriation, and thereby also every other previous mode of appropriation. They have nothing of their own to secure and to fortify; their mission is to destroy all previous securities for, and insurances of, individual property.

All previous historical movements were movements of minorities, or in the interest of minorities. The proletarian movement is the self-conscious, independent movement of the immense majority, in the interest of the immense majority. The proletariat, the lowest stratum of our present society, cannot stir, cannot raise itself up, without the whole superincumbent strata of official society being sprung into the air.

Though not in substance, yet in form, the struggle of the proletariat with the bourgeoisie is at first a national struggle. The proletariat of each country must, of course, first of all settle matters with its own bourgeoisie.

In depicting the most general phases of the development of the proletariat, we traced the more or less veiled civil war, raging within existing society, up to the point where that war breaks out into open revolution, and where the violent overthrow of the bourgeoisie lays the foundation for the sway of the proletariat.

Hitherto, every form of society has been based, as we have already seen, on the antagonism of oppressing and opressed classes. But in order to oppress a class, certain conditions must be assured to it under which it can, at least, continue its slavish existence. The serf, in the period of serfdom, raised himself to membership in the commune, just as the petty bourgeois, under the yoke of feudal absolutism, managed to develop into a bourgeois. The modern laborer, on the contrary, instead of rising with the progress of industry, sinks deeper and deeper below the conditions of existence of his own class. He becomes a pauper, and pauperism develops more rapidly than population and wealth. And here it becomes evident, that the bourgeoisie is unfit any longer to be the ruling class in society, and to impose its conditions of existence upon society as an over-riding law. It is unfit to rule, because it is incompetent to assure an existence to its slave within his slavery, because it cannot help letting him sink into such a state that it has to feed him, instead of being fed by him. Society can no longer live under this bourgeoisie, in other words, its existence is no longer compatible with society.

The essential condition for the existence, and for the sway of the bourgeois class, is the formation and augmentation of capital;

the condition for capital is wage-labor. Wage labor rests exclusively on competition between the laborers. The advance of industry, whose involuntary promoter is the bourgeoisie, replaces the isolation of the laborers, due to competition, by their revolutionary combination, due to association. The development of Modern Industry, therefore, cuts from under its feet the very foundation on which the bourgeoisie produces and appropriates products. What the bourgeoisie therefore produces, above all, are its own grave-diggers. Its fall and the victory of the proletariat are equally inevitable.

II. PROLETARIANS AND COMMUNISTS

In what relation do the Communists stand to the proletarians as a whole?

The Communists do not form a separate party opposed to other working-class parties.

They have no interests separate and apart from those of the proletariat as a whole.

They do not set up any sectarian principles of their own, by which to shape and mould the proletarian movement.

The Communists are distinguished from the other working class parties by this only: 1. In the national struggles of the proletarians of the different countries, they point out and bring to the front the common interests of the entire proletariat independently of all nationality. 2. In the various stages of development which the struggle of the working class against the bourgeoisie has to pass through, they always and everywhere represent the interests of the movement as a whole.

The Communists, therefore, are on the one hand, practically, the most advanced and resolute section of the working class parties of every country, that section which pushes forward all others; on the other hand, theoretically, they have over the great mass of the proletariat the advantage of clearly understanding the line of march, the conditions, and the ultimate general results of the proletarian movement.

The immediate aim of the Communists is the same as that of all the other proletarian parties; formation of the proletariat into a class, overthrow of the bourgeois supremacy, conquest of political power by the proletariat.

The theoretical conclusions of the Communists are in no way

based on ideas or principles that have been invented, or discovered, by this or that would-be universal reformer.

They merely express, in general terms, actual relations springing from an existing class struggle, from a historical movement going on under our very eyes. The abolition of existing property relations is not at all a distinctive feature of Communism.

All property relations in the past have continually been subject to historical change consequent upon the change in historical conditions.

The French Revolution, for example, abolished feudal property in favor of bourgeois property.

The distinguishing feature of Communism is not the abolition of property generally, but the abolition of bourgeois property. But modern bourgeois private property is the final and most complete expression of the system of producing and appropriating products, that is based on class antagonism, on the exploitation of the many by the few.

In this sense, the theory of the Communists may be summed up in the single sentence: Abolition of private property.

We Communists have been reproached with the desire of abolishing the right of personally acquiring property as the fruit of a man's own labor, which property is alleged to be the ground work of all personal freedom, activity and independence.

Hard-won, self-acquired, self-earned property! Do you mean the property of the petty artisan and of the small peasant, a form of property that preceded the bourgeois form? There is no need to abolish that; the development of industry has to a great extent already destroyed it, and is still destroying it daily.

Or do you mean modern bourgeois private property?

But does wage-labor create any property for the laborer? Not a bit. It creates capital, i.e., that kind of property which exploits wage-labor, and which cannot increase except upon condition of getting a new supply of wage-labor for fresh exploitation. Property, in its present form, is based on the antagonism of capital and wage-labor. Let us examine both sides of this antagonism.

To be a capitalist, is to have not only a purely personal, but a social status in production. Capital is a collective product, and only by the united action of many members, nay, in the last resort, only by the united action of all members of society, can it be set in motion.

Capital is therefore not a personal, it is a social power.

When, therefore, capital is converted into common property, into the property of all members of society, personal property is not thereby transformed into social property. It is only the social character of the property that is changed. It loses its class-character.

Let us now take wage-labor.

The average price of wage-labor is the minimum wage, i.e., that quantum of the means of subsistence, which is absolutely requisite to keep the laborer in bare existence as a laborer. What, therefore, the wage-laborer appropriates by means of his labor, merely suffices to prolong and reproduce a bare existence. We by no means intend to abolish this personal appropriation of the products of labor, an appropriation that is made for the maintenance and reproduction of human life, and that leaves no surplus where with to command the labor of others. All that we want to do away with is the miserable character of this appropriation, under which the laborer lives merely to increase capital, and is allowed to live only in so far as the interest of the ruling class requires it.

In bourgeois society, living labor is but a means to increase accumulated labor. In communist society, accumulated labor is but a means to widen, to enrich, to promote the existence of the laborer.

In bourgeois society, therefore, the past dominates the present; in communist society, the present dominates the past. In bourgeois society capital is independent and has individuality, while the living person is dependent and has no individuality.

And the abolition of this state of things is called by the bourgeois, abolition of individuality and freedom! And rightly so. The aboliton of bourgeois individuality, bourgeois independence, and bourgeois freedom is undoubtedly aimed at.

By freedom is meant, under the present bourgeois conditions of production, free trade, free selling and buying.

But if selling and buying disappears, free selling and buying disappears also. This talk about free selling and buying, and all the other "brave words" of our bourgeoisie about freedom in general, have a meaning, if any, only in contrast with restricted selling and buying, with the fettered traders of the Middle Ages, but have no meaning when opposed to the Communistic abolition of buying and selling, of the bourgeois conditions of production, and of the bourgeoisie itself.

You are horrified at our intending to do away with private property. But in your existing society, private property is already done away with for nine-tenths of the population; its existence for the few is solely due to its non-existence in the hands of those nine-tenths. You reproach us, therefore, with intending to do away with a form of property, the necessary condition for whose existence is, the non-existence of any property for the immense majority of society.

In one word, you reproach us with intending to do away with your property. Precisely so; that is just what we intend.

From the moment when labor can no longer be converted into capital, money, or rent, into a social power capable of being monopolized, i.e., from the moment when individual property can no longer be transformed into bourgeois property, into capital, from that moment, you say, individuality vanishes.

You must, therefore, confess that by "individual" you mean no other person than the bourgeois, than the middle-class owner of property. This person must, indeed, be swept out of the way, and made impossible.

Communism deprives no man of the power to appropriate the products of society: all that it does is to deprive him of the power to subjugate the labor of others by means of such appropriation.

It has been objected, that upon the abolition of private property all work will cease, and universal laziness will overtake us.

According to this, bourgeois society ought long ago to have gone to the dogs through sheer idleness; for those of its members who work, acquire nothing, and those who acquire anything, do not work. The whole of this objection is but another expression of the tautology: that there can no longer be any wage-labor when there is no longer any capital.

All objections urged against the Communistic mode of producing and appropriating material products have, in the same way, been urged against the Communistic modes of producing and appropriating intellectual products. Just as, to the bourgeois, the disappearance of class property is the disappearance of production itself, so the disappearance of class culture is to him identical with the disappearance of all culture.

That culture, the loss of which he laments, is, for the enormous majority, a mere training to act as a machine.

But don't wrangle with us so long as you apply, to our intended abolition of bourgeois property, the standard of your bourgeois notions of freedom, culture, law, etc. Your very ideas are but the outgrowth of the conditions of your bourgeois production and bourgeois property, just as your jurisprudence is but the will of your class made into a law for all, a will, whose essential character and direction are determined by the economic conditions of existence of your class.

The selfish misconception that induces you to transform into eternal laws of nature and of reason, the social forms springing from your present mode of production and form of property—historical relations that rise and disappear in the progress of production—this misconception you share with every ruling class that has preceded you. What you see clearly in the case of ancient property, what you admit in the case of feudal property, you are of course forbidden to admit in the case of your own bourgeois form of property.

Abolition of the family! Even the most radical flare up at this infamous proposal of the Communists.

On what foundation is the present family, the bourgeois family, based? On capital, on private gain. In its completely developed form this family exists only among the bourgeoisie. But this state of things finds its complement in the practical absence of the family among the proletarians, and in public prostitution.

The bourgeois family will vanish as a matter of course when its complement vanishes, and both will vanish with the vanishing of capital.

Do you charge us with wanting to stop the exploitation of children by their parents? To this crime we plead guilty.

But, you will say, we destroy the most hallowed of relations, when we replace home education by social.

And your education! Is not that also social, and determined by the social conditions under which you educate, by the intervention, direct or indirect, of society by means of schools, etc? The Communists have not invented the intervention of society in education; they do but seek to alter the character of that intervention, and to rescue education from the influence of the ruling class.

The bourgeois clap-trap about the family and education, about the hallowed co-relation of parent and child, becomes all the more disgusting, the more, by the action of Modern Industry, all family ties among the proletarians are torn asunder, and their children transformed into simple articles of commerce and instruments of labor.

But you Communists would introduce community of women, screams the whole bourgeoisie in chorus.

The bourgeois sees in his wife a mere instrument of production. He hears that the instruments of production are to be exploited in common, and, naturally, can come to no other conclusion, than that the lot of being common to all will likewise fall to the women.

He has not even a suspicion that the real point aimed at is to do away 'with the status of women as mere instruments of production.

For the rest, nothing is more ridiculous than the virtuous indignation of our bourgeois at the community of women which, they pretend, is to be openly and officially established by the Communists. The Communists have no need to introduce community of women; it has existed almost from time immemorial.

Our bourgeois, not content with having the wives and daughters of their proletarians at their disposal, not to speak of common prostitutes, take the greatest pleasure in seducing each other's wives.

Bourgeois marriage is in reality a system of wives in common and thus, at the most, what the Communists might possibly be reproached with, is that they desire to introduce, in substitution for a hypocritically concealed, an openly legalized community of women. For the rest, it is self-evident, that the abolition of the present system of production must bring with it the abolition of the community of women springing from the system, i.e., of prostitution both public and private.

The Communists are further reproached with desiring to abolish countries and nationalities.

The working men have no country. We cannot take from them what they have not got. Since the proletariat must first of all acquire political supremacy, must rise to the leading class of the nation, must constitute itself the nation, it is, so far, itself national, though not in the bourgeois sense of the word.

National differences, and antagonisms between peoples, are daily more and more vanishing, owing to the development of the bourgeoisie, to freedom of commerce, to the world-market, to uniformity in the mode of production and in the conditions of life corresponding thereto.

The supremacy of the proletariat will cause them to vanish still faster. United action, of the leading civilized countries at least, is one of the first conditions for the emancipation of the proletariat.

In proportion as the exploitation of one individual by another is put an end to, the exploitation of one nation by another will also be put an end to. In proportion as the antagonism between classes within the nation vanishes, the hostility of one nation to another will come to an end.

The charges against Communism made from a religious, a philosophical, and generally, from an ideological standpoint, are not deserving of serious examination.

Does it require deep intuition to comprehend that man's ideas, views, and conceptions, in one word, man's consciousness, changes with every change in the conditions of his material existence, in his social relations and in his social life?

What else does the history of ideas prove, than that intellectual production changes in character in proportion as material production is changed? The ruling ideas of each age have ever been the ideas of its ruling class.

When people speak of ideas that revolutionize society, they do but express the fact, that within the old society, the elements of a new one have been created, and that the dissolution of the old ideas keeps even pace with the dissolution of the old conditions of existence.

When the ancient world was in its last throes, the ancient religions were overcome by Christianity. When Christian ideas succumbed in the 18th century to rationalist ideas, feudal society fought its death-battle with the then revolutionary bourgeoisie. The ideas of religious liberty and freedom of conscience, merely gave expression to the sway of free competition within the domain of knowledge.

"Undoubtedly," it will be said, "religious, moral, philosophical, and juridical ideas have been modified in the course of historical development. But religion, morality, philosophy, political science and law, constantly survived this change.

"There are, besides, eternal truths, such as Freedom, Justice, etc., that are common to all states of society. But Communism abolishes eternal truths, it abolishes all religion, and all morality, instead of constituting them on a new basis; it therefore acts in contradiction to all past historical experience."

What does this accusation reduce itself to? The history of all past society has consisted in the development of class antagonisms, antagonisms that assumed different forms at different epochs.

But whatever form they may have taken, one fact is common to all past ages, viz., the exploitation of one part of society by the other. No wonder, then, that the social consciousness of past ages, despite all the multiplicity and variety it displays, moves within certain common forms, or general ideas, which can not completely vanish except with the total disappearance of class antagonisms.

The Communist revolution is the most radical rupture with traditional property-relations; no wonder that its development involves the most radical rupture with traditional ideas.

But let us have done with the bourgeois objections to Communism.

We have seen above that the first step in the revolution by the working class is to raise the proletariat to the position of ruling class, to win the battle of democracy.

The proletariat will use its political supremacy, to wrest, by degrees, all capital from the bourgeoisie, to centralize all instruments of production in the hands of the State, i.e., of the proletariat organized as the ruling class; and to increase the total of productive forces as rapidly as possible.

Of course, in the beginning, this cannot be effected except by means of despotic inroads on the rights of property, and on the conditions of bourgeois production; by means of measures, therefore, which appear economically insufficient and untenable, but which, in the course of the movement, outstrip themselves, necessitate further inroads upon the old social order, and are unavoidable as a means of entirely revolutionizing the mode of production.

These measures will of course be different in different countries.

Nevertheless in the most advanced countries the following will be pretty generally applicable:

1. Abolition of property in land and application of all rents of land to public purposes.

2. A heavy progressive or graduated income tax.

3. Abolition of all right of inheritance.

4. Confiscation of the property of all emigrants and rebels.

5. Centralization of credit in the hands of the State, by means of a national bank with State capital and an exclusive monopoly.

6. Centralization of the means of communication and transport in the hands of the State.

7. Extension of factories and instruments of production owned by the State; the bringing into cultivation of waste lands, and the improvement of the soil generally in accordance with a common plan.

8. Equal liability of all to labor. Establishment of industrial armies, especially for agriculture.

9. Combination of agriculture with manufacturing industries; gradual abolition of the distinction between town and country, by a more equable distribution of population over the country.

10. Free education for all children in public schools. Abolition of children's factory labor in its present form. Combination of education with industrial production, etc., etc.

When, in the course of development, class distinctions have disappeared, and all production has been concentrated in the hands of a vast association of the whole nation, the public power will lose its political character. Political power, properly so called, is merely the organized power of one class for oppressing another. If the proletariat durings its contest with the bourgeoisie is compelled, by the force of circumstances, to organize itself as a class, if, by means of a revolution, it makes itself the ruling class, and, as such, sweeps away by force the old conditions of production, then it will, along with these conditions, have swept away the conditions for the existence of class antagonisms, and of classes generally, and will thereby have abolished its own supremacy as a class.

In place of the old bourgeois society, with its classes and class antagonisms, we shall have an association, in which the free development of each is the condition for the free development of all.

III.   SOCIALIST AND COMMUNIST LITERATURE

3. *Critical-Utopian Socialism and Communism*

We do not here refer to that literature which, in every great modern revolution, has always given voice to the demands of the proletariat: such as the writings of Babeuf and others.

The first direct attempts of the proletariat to attain its own ends, made in times of universal excitement, when feudal society was being overthrown, these attempts necessarily failed, owing to the then undeveloped state of the proletariat, as well as to the absence of the economic conditions for its emancipation, conditions that had yet to be produced, and could be produced by the impending bourgeois epoch alone. The revolutionary literature that accompanied these first movements of the proletariat had necessarily a reactionary character. It inculcated universal asceticism and social levelling in its crudest form.

The socialist and communist systems properly so called, those of St. Simon, Fourier, Owen and others, spring into existence in the early undeveloped period, described above, of the struggle between proletariat and bourgeoisie. . . .

The undeveloped state of the class struggle, as well as their own surroundings, causes Socialists of this kind to consider themselves far superior to all class antagonisms. They want to improve the condition of every member of society, even that of the most favored. Hence, they habitually appeal to society at large, without distinction of class; nay, by preference, to the ruling class. For how can people, when once they understand their system, fail to see in it the best possible plan of the best possible state of society?

Hence, they reject all political, and especially all revolutionary action; they wish to attain their ends by peaceful means, and endeavor, by small experiments, necessarily doomed to failure, and by the force of example, to pave the way for the new social Gospel.

Such phantastic pictures of future society, painted at a time when the proletariat is still in a very undeveloped state, and has but a phantastic conception of its own position, correspond with the first instinctive yearnings of that class for a general reconstruction of society.

But these Socialist and Communist publications contain also a critical element. They attack every principle of existing society.

Hence they are full of the most valuable materials for the enlightenment of the working class. The practical measures proposed in them, such as the abolition of the distinction between town and country, of the family, of the carrying on of industries for the account of private individuals and of the wage-system; the proclamation of social harmony; the conversion of the functions of the State into a mere superintendence of production—all these proposals point solely to the disappearance of class-antagonisms which were, at that time only just cropping up, and which, in these publications, are recognised in their earliest, indistinct, and undefined forms only. These proposals, therefore, are of a purely Utopian character.

The significance of Critical-Utopian Socialism and Communism bears an inverse relation to historical development. In proportion as the modern class struggle develops and takes definite shape, this phantastic standing apart from the contest, these phantastic attacks on it, lose all practical value and all theoretical justification. Therefore, although the originators of these systems were, in many respects, revolutionary, their disciples have, in every case, formed mere reactionary sects. They hold fast by the original views of their masters, in opposition to the progressive historical development of the proletariat. They, therefore, endeavor, and that consistently, to deaden the class struggle and to reconcile the class antagonisms. They still dream of experimental realisation of their social Utopias, of founding isolated *phalansteres,* of establishing "Home Colonies," of setting up a "Little Icaria"—duodecima editions of the New Jerusalem and to realize all these castles in the air, they are compelled to appeal to the feelings and purses of the bourgeois. By degrees they sink into the category of the reactionary conservative Socialists depicted above, differing from these only by more systematic pedantry, and by their fanatical and superstitious belief in the miraculous effects of their social science.

They, therefore, violently oppose all political action on the part of the working class; such action, according to them, can only result from blind unbelief in the new Gospel. . . .

IV. POSITION OF THE COMMUNISTS IN RELATION TO THE
VARIOUS EXISTING OPPOSITION PARTIES

Section II has made clear the relations of the Communists

to the existing working class parties, such as the Chartists in England and the Agrarian Reformers in America.

The Communists fight for the attainment of the immediate aims, for the enforcement of the momentary interests of the working class; but in the movement of the present, they also represent and take care of the future of that movement. In France the Communists ally themselves with the Social-Democrats, reserving however, the right to take up a critical position in regard to phrases and illusions traditionally handed down from the great Revolution.

In Switzerland they support the Radicals, without losing sight of the fact that this party consists of antagonistic elements, partly of Democratic Socialists, in the French sense, partly of radical bourgeois.

In Poland they support the party that insists on an agrarian revolution, as the prime condition of national emancipation, that party which fomented the insurrection of Cracow in 1846.

In Germany they fight with the bourgeoisie whenever it acts in a revolutionary way, against the absolute monarchy, the feudal squirearchy, and the petty bourgeoisie.

But they never cease, for a single instant, to instill into the working class the clearest possible recognition of the hostile antagonism between bourgeoisie and proletariat, in order that the German workers may straightway use, as so many weapons against the bourgeoisie, the social and political conditions that the bourgeoisie must necessarily introduce along with its supremacy, and in order that, after the fall of the reactionary classes in Germany, the fight against the bourgeoisie itself may immediately begin.

The Communists turn their attention chiefly to Germany, because that country is on the eve of a bourgeois revolution, that is bound to be carried out under more advanced conditions of European civilization, and with a more developed proletariat, than that of England was in the seventeenth, and of France in the eighteenth century, and because the bourgeois revolution in Germany will be but the prelude to an immediately following proletarian revolution.

In short, the Communists everywhere support every revolutionary movement against the existing social and political order of things.

In all these movements they bring to the front, as the leading question in each, the property question, no matter what its degree of development at the time.

Finally, they labor everywhere for the union and agreement of the democratic parties of all countries.

The Communists disdain to conceal their views and aims. They openly declare that their ends can be attained only by the forcible overthrow of all existing social conditions. Let the ruling classes tremble at a Communistic revolution. The proletarians have nothing to lose but their chains. They have a world to win.

Working men of all countries, unite!

THE POETS

Alfred, Lord Tennyson (1809-1892)

NORTHERN FARMER

(New Style)

Dosn't thou 'ear my 'erse's legs, as they canters awaay?
Proputty, proputty, proputty—that's what I 'ears 'em saay.
Proputty, proputty, proputty—Sam, thou's an ass for thy pains;
Theer's moor sense i' one o' 'is legs, nor in all thy brains.

Woa—theer's a craw to pluck wi' tha, Sam: yon's parson's 'ouse—
Dosn't thou know that a man mun be eather a man or a mouse?
Time to think on it then; for thou'll be twenty to weeak.
Proputty, proputty—woa then, woa—let ma 'ear mysen speak.

Me an' thy muther, Sammy, 'as bean a-talkin' o' thee;
Thou's bean talkin' to muther, an' she bean a-tellin' it me.
Thou'll not marry for munny—thou's sweet upo' parson's lass—
Noa—thou'll marry for luvv—an' we boath on us thinks tha an ass.

Seea'd her to-daay goa by—Saaint's daay—they was ringing
    the bells.
She's a beauty, thou thinks—an' soa is scoors o' gells,
Them as 'as munny an' all—wot's a beauty?—the flower as blaws.
But proputty, proputty sticks, an' proputty, proputty graws.

Do'ant be stunt; taake time. I knaws what maakes tha sa mad.
Warn't I craazed fur the lasses mysen when I wur a lad?
But I knaw'd a Quaaker feller as often 'as towd ma this:
'Doant thou marry for munny, but goa wheer munny is!"

An' I went wheer munny war; an' thy muther coom to 'and,
Wi' lots o' munny laaid by, an' a nicetish bit o' land.
Maaybe she warn't a beauty—I niver giv it a thowt—
But warn't she as good to cuddle an' kiss as a lass as 'ant nowt?

Parson's lass 'ant nowt, an' she weant 'a nowt when 'e 's dead,
Mun be a guvness, lad, or summut, and addle her bread.
Why? fur 'e 's nobbut a curate, an' weant niver get hissen clear,
An' 'e maade the bed as 'e ligs on afoor 'e coom'd to the shere.

An' thin 'e coom'd to the parish wi' lots o' Varsity debt,
Stook to his taail they did, an' 'e 'ant got shut on 'em yet.
An' e' ligs on 'is back i' the grip, wi' noan to lend 'im a shove,
Woorse nor a far welter'd yowe; fur, Sammy, 'e maried fur luvv.

Luvv? What's luvv? thou can luvv thy lass an' 'er munny too,
Maakin' 'em goa togither, as they've good right to do.
Couldn' I luvv thy muther by cause o' 'er munny laaid by?
Naay—fur I luvv'd 'er a vast sight moor fur it; reason why.

Ay, an' thy muther says thou wants to marry the lass,
Cooms of a gentleman burn; an' we boath on us thinks tha an ass.
Woa then, proputty, wilthah?—an ass as near as mays nowt—
Woa then, wiltha? dangtha!—the bees is as fell as owt.

Break me a bit o' the esh for his 'ead, lad, out o' the fence!
Gentleman burn! what's gentleman burn? is it shillins an' pence?
Proputty, proputty's ivrything 'ere, an', Sammy, I'm blest
If it isn't the saame ooop yonder, fur them as 'as it's the best.

Tis'n them as 'as munny as breaks into 'ouses an' steals,
Them as 'as coats to their backs an' taakes their regular meals.
Noa, but it's them as niver knaws wheer a meal's to be 'ad.
Taake my word for it, Sammy, the poor in a loomp is bad.

Them or thir feythers, tha sees, mun a' bean a laazy lot,
Fur work mun 'a gone to the gittin' whiniver munny was got.
Feyther 'ad ammost nowt; least ways his munny was 'id
But 'e tued an' moil'd issen dead, an' 'e died a good un, 'e did.

Look thou theer wheer Wrigglesby beck cooms out by the 'ill!
Feyther run oop to the farm, an' I runs oop to the mill;
An' I'll run oop to the brig, an' that thou'll live to see;
And if thou marries a good un I'll leave the land to thee.

Thim's my noations, Sammy, wheerby I means to stick;
But if thou marries a bad un, I'll leave the land to Dick.
Coom oop, proputty, proputty—that's what I 'ears 'im saay—
Proputty, proputty, proputty—canter an' canter awaay.

Arthur Hugh Clough (1819-1861)

THE LATEST DECALOGUE

Thou shalt have one God only; who
Would be at the expense of two?
No graven images may be
Worshiped, except the currency:
Swear not at all; for, for thy curse
Thine enemy is none the worse:
At church on Sunday to attend
Will serve to keep the world thy friend:
Honor thy parents: that is, all
From whom advancement may befall;
Thou shalt not kill; but need'st not strive
Officiously to keep alive:
Do not adultery commit;
Advantage rarely comes of it:
Thou shalt not steal; an empty feat,
When it's so lucrative to cheat:
Bear not false witness; let the lie
Have time on its own wings to fly:
Thou shalt not covet, but tradition
Approves all forms of competition.

From DIPSYCHUS

As I sat at the cafe, I said to myself,
They may talk as they please about what they call pelf,
They may sneer as they like about eating and drinking,
But help it I cannot, I cannot help thinking,
  How pleasant it is to have money, heigh ho!
  How pleasant it is to have money.

I sit at my table en grand seigneur,
And when I have done, throw a crust to the poor;
Not only the pleasure, one's self, of good living,
But also the pleasure of now and then giving.
  So pleasant it is to have money, heigh ho!
  So pleasant it is to have money. . . .

I drive through the streets, and I care not a d—n;
  The people they stare, and they ask who I am;
And if I should chance to run over a cad,
I can pay for the damage if ever so bad.
    So pleasant it is to have money, heigh ho!
    So pleasant it is to have money.

We stroll to our box and look down on the pit,
And if it weren't low should be tempted to spit;
We loll and we talk until people look up,
And when it's half over we go out to sup.
    So pleasant it is to have money, heigh ho!
    So pleasant it is to have money.

The best of the tables and best of the fare—
And as for the others, the devil may care;
It isn't our fault if they dare not afford
To sup like a prince and be drunk as a lord.
    So pleasant it is to have money, heigh ho!
    So pleasant it is to have money.

Thomas Hood (1799-1845)

THE SONG OF THE SHIRT

With fingers weary and worn,
  With eyelids heavy and red,
A woman sat in unwomanly rags,
  Plying her needle and thread—
    Stitch! stitch! stitch!
In poverty, hunger, and dirt,
  And still with a voice of dolorous pitch
She sang the "Song of the Shirt!"

  "Work! work! work!
While the cock is crowing aloof!
  And work—work—work,
Till the stars shine through the roof!

It's O! to be a slave
  Along with the barbarous Turk,
Where woman has never a soul to save,
  If this is Christian work!

  "Work—work—work
Till the brain begins to swim!
  Work—work—work
Till the eyes are heavy and dim!
Seam, and gusset, and band,
  Band, and gusset, and seam,
Till over the buttons I fall asleep,
  And sew them on in a dream!

"O, men, with sisters dear!
  O, men, with mothers and wives!
It is not linen you're wearing out,
  But human creatures' lives!
    Stitch—stitch—stitch,
  In poverty, hunger, and dirt,
Sewing at once, with a double thread,
  A shroud as well as a shirt.

"But why do I talk of death?
  That phantom of grisly bone,
I hardly fear his terrible shape,
  It seems so like my own—
It seems so like my own,
  Because of the fasts I keep;
O, God! that bread should be so dear,
  And flesh and blood so cheap!

"Work—work—work!
  My labor never flags;
And what are its wages? A bed of straw,
  A crust of bread—and rags.
That shattered roof—and this naked floor—
  A table—a broken chair—
And a wall so blank, my shadow I thank
  For sometimes falling there!

"Work—work—work!
   From weary chime to chime,
Work—work—work,
   As prisoners work for crime!
Band, and gusset, and seam,
   Seam, and gusset, and band,
Till the heart is sick, and the brain benumbed,
   As well as the weary hand.

"Work—work—work,
In the dull December light,
   And work—work—work,
When the weather is warm and bright—
While underneath the eaves
   The brooding swallows cling,
As if to show me their sunny backs,
   And twit me with the spring.

"O! but to breathe the breath
Of the cowslip and primrose sweet—
   With the sky above my head,
And the grass beneath my feet,
For only one short hour
   To feel as I used to feel,
Before I knew the woes of want,
   And the walk that costs a meal!

"O! but for one short hour!
   A respite however brief!
No blessed leisure for love or hope,
   But only time for grief!
A little weeping would ease my heart,
   But in their briny bed
My tears must stop, for every drop
   Hinders needle and thread!"

With fingers weary and worn,
  With eyelids heavy and red,
A woman sat in unwomanly rags,
  Plying her needle and thread—
    Stitch! stitch! stitch!
  In poverty, hunger, and dirt,
And still with a voice of dolorous pitch,—
Would that its tone could reach the rich!—
  She sang this "Song of the Shirt!"

Eugene Pottier (1816-1887)

THE INTERNATIONAL

Arise, ye pris'ners of starvation!
  Arise, ye wretched of the earth,
For Justice thunders condemnation,
  A better world's in birth.
No more tradition's chain shall bind us.
  Arise, ye slaves; No more in thrall!
The earth shall rise on new foundations,
  We have been naught, we shall be all.

Refrain:

  'Tis the final conflict,
    Let each stand in his place,
  The International Party
    Shall be the human race.

SELECTED ANN ARBOR PAPERBACKS

works of enduring merit

For a complete list of Ann Arbor Paperback titles write:
THE UNIVERSITY OF MICHIGAN PRESS / ANN ARBOR